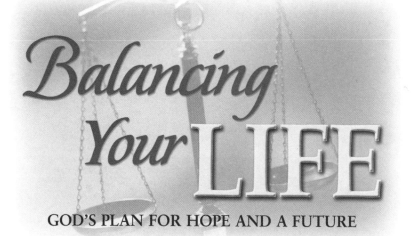

Balancing Your LIFE

GOD'S PLAN FOR HOPE AND A FUTURE

THOMAS NELSON PUBLISHERS®

Nashville

Balancing Your LIFE

GOD'S PLAN FOR HOPE AND A FUTURE

Suzan D. Johnson Cook

THOMAS NELSON PUBLISHERS®
Nashville

Published by Thomas Nelson, Inc.
P.O. Box 141000
Nashville, TN 37214

Library of Congress Cataloguing-in-Publication Data is available.

ISBN: 0-7852-5070-0

Printed in United States

03 04 05 06 07 – 5 4 3 2 1

Foreword

If you are going to be a leading lady for the long term, one of the things you will have to cultivate in the garden of your life is balance. If you are going to last in the light of your destiny, you need to be strong and healthy and whole — and you'll achieve that by gaining and maintaining balance physically, mentally, and spiritually.

I know of no one better qualified to speak to women about issues of life balance than Dr. Suzan Johnson Cook. This leading lady balances with finesse her various roles as wife, mother, senior pastor, and president of the Hampton University Ministers Conference — the world's largest gathering of African American clergy. She is creative and compassionate, savvy and sensational, electrifying and inspirational. I am delighted to commend her to you as she teaches you the valuable lessons she has learned.

In order to help you get started on your journey toward a balanced life, I'd like to take a moment to walk you through each of the features you will find in the pages of this workbook so that you will understand why we have included them and what I hope your interaction with them will accomplish in your life.

Introducing . . ..· The word speaks for itself. Introductions to each chapter will simply show you the big picture of the subject covered and give you a glimpse of where we are headed in that chapter.

The Main Event: I am delighted by the wealth of sound, practical advice and godly wisdom in this workbook. This helpful information is presented to you in sections entitled "The Main Event," which is divided into "Acts," just as a stage play is divided into acts. Each act focuses specifically on a particular aspect of the larger subject of the chapter.

You're On: As you work through this book, I hope you will find many ways to apply the information to your own life. To help you, we have included some questions for you to answer. I hope you'll think about them, answer them, and even use an extra sheet of paper or your journal if you find yourself wanting to respond to them more extensively.

Learn Your Lines: You probably know that God's Word is "living and active," as we read in the Book of Hebrews, but I want you to continue to experience its transforming power in your daily life. Therefore at the end of many acts, you will find several scriptures relating to the subject you have just studied. As the Word gets worked into your mind, it gets worked out in your life, so I believe these scriptures really are keys to help you unlock personal victory and success.

Supporting Roles: This particular workbook contains some valuable information on important health issues, such as heart disease, breast cancer, diabetes, and others. In these chapters, found in Section 2, we have replaced "Learn Your Lines" with a feature entitled "Supporting Roles," which lists websites or other sources where you can find out more about these topics.

Coming Soon: I love this part of the workbook because it is your opportunity to dream on paper. These beautifully designed pages at the end of each chapter will allow you to sum up what you have learned throughout that chapter, and imagine how you will apply these lessons. Take time to really think about your life, your hopes, aspirations, and inspirations as you put them into written form.

Action!: Goal-setting is so important to successful living that we have concluded every chapter with space for you to list specific goals pertaining to the topic of that chapter. I encourage you to use that space to set a few measurable, challenging, attainable goals and to give yourself a deadline and a reward for reaching each one. In the back of the workbook you will find an Appendix where you can prioritize all your goals together on one list.

Leading Lady, the lights are coming up, and it is time for you to shine. I hope you will enjoy this workbook and that it will help you keep your balance in every area of life as you take your place on life's center stage.

God bless you,
T. D. Jakes

Contents

Introduction

The year was 1992, and I sat in front of Kentucky Fried Chicken restaurant with the man who is now my husband. I had been waiting on the Lord, fasting and praying for Him to bring the right man into my life. Brother Cook had been doing the same, and so, on the Monday of Holy Week, the two of us went on our first date.

As we talked that evening, Brother Cook said to me, "I have a theory; it's called the PEMS theory. I want to take care of you **P**hysically, **E**motionally, **M**entally, and **S**piritually." Can you imagine what I thought when I heard those words? All right now! This was a man worth spending time with!

Leading lady, Brother Cook was on to something. He understood that there are many pieces to our lives and that we must pay attention to each one and keep them all in balance. I believe the apostle Paul also understood how critical it is to attend to every aspect of our lives when he wrote these words: "Now may the God of peace Himself sanctify you completely; and may your whole *spirit, soul* and *body* be preserved blameless at the coming of our Lord Jesus Christ" (1 Thess. 5:23, italics mine).

As we go through this workbook together, I will share portions of my personal journey with you. But for now, let me say that I have learned how important it is to take care of myself physically, mentally, and spiritually — and I want to help you take care of yourself, too. Do you know that your health is your greatest asset? It is, and taking care of yourself and staying healthy are all about achieving balance and making sure that one area of life does not dominate while others are neglected.

You know what happens when something is off-balance, don't you? It keeps leaning until it topples over! I don't want that to happen to you. I want you to be able to stand up straight and to walk strong! So, in the pages of this book I've offered some of the most sound, practical advice I can give you. I'm delighted to share with you many of the life lessons I learned the hard way, hoping to spare you some of the mistakes I've made and to encourage you to try some of the things that worked.

You are a leading lady, and the rest of your life is ahead of you. You'll need to be strong and balanced as you fulfill all of the wonderful plans God has for your life. So, as you begin the process of becoming healthier and more whole, I echo an ancient prayer for you: "Beloved, I pray that you may prosper in all things and be in health, just as your soul prospers" (3 John 2).

Are you ready? Let's walk on together — and let the journey begin!

Big
Picture
Balance

1

The Lady Learns to Balance

Introducing

ave you ever stopped to think about the miracle that you are? I mean it — you are an intricate and beautiful creation. Like all of God's children, you are a complex weave of physical structure and functions, emotional tendencies, mental aptitudes, and spiritual capacities. You are made in the very image of God, and He knew what He was doing when He made you just the way you are. Now, I know there are days you don't feel that way, but we leading ladies believe the truth of God's Word above our circumstances, don't we? And the Word says, "Then God said, 'Let Us make man in Our image, according to Our likeness;' . . . So God created man in His own image; in the image of God He created him; male and female He created them" (Gen. 1:26, 27).

The Bible also says that you are "fearfully and wonderfully made" and that God Himself "formed [your] inward parts" (Ps. 139:13, 14). He breathed into your nostrils the breath of life, causing you to spring to life and grace the earth with your presence. You are uniquely fashioned as God's handiwork, and you are more than just your physical body. You are body, mind, and spirit. Each part is important, and in order for you to function at your best, all three must flow together. In this chapter, I'd like to help you identify any aspects of your life that may be out of balance and help you re-gain your stability so that you can walk through your life steady and strong, living every day to the fullest.

The Main Event

Act 1: Getting Your Balance

You know by now that I want to help you gain balance in the areas of your body, your mind and your spiritual life. Like you, I have known and observed many women who are off-balance: they overemphasize one aspect of their lives while virtually discounting the others. You know what I mean.

> *You are body, mind, and spirit. Each part is important, and in order for you to function at your optimum, all three must flow together.*

There are those women who focus on their bodies, without feeding or exercising their minds or working on their spiritual lives. They are tight and toned, but may not have read a book in the last ten years. They have perfectly coiffed hair and manicured nails, but may have a closer relationship with the beautician than with the Lord.

Then there are those who pursue the things of the mind. They may be reading three books — on various subjects — all at the same time, but may be ingesting fast food as quickly as they devour information. They may be up-to-the-minute on world events, but completely ignorant of what the Lord is doing in their own lives.

Finally, we all know some super-spiritual sisters, the ones who are so spiritual that they are no earthly good, as the old saying goes. Every sentence includes a "Hallelujah!" But for every time that word crosses those lips, so does a piece of homemade pie. They'd love to dance before the Lord, but seem to only be able to waddle. They pray about everything, but rarely employ wisdom or common sense.

Have I stepped on your toes, my sister? Are you one of the women I have just described? If so, be encouraged! You're in the right place and you'll find help in the pages of this workbook. As you can see, when any one of these elements (body, mind, or spirit) begins to dominate the others — or when one is neglected—a person ends up out of balance, which can lead to confusion, frustration, and even disease. Not maintaining balance is like dissing yourself — and I know you don't want to do that. Chances are you may already see the need to make some adjustments in your life. Balance is possible, but lasting change does not happen overnight; it is a process. Personal wholeness is only possible when all three aspects of life are carrying the appropriate amount of weight and rightly related to each other.

> *Personal wholeness is only possible when all three aspects of life are carrying the appropriate amount of weight and rightly related to each other.*

You're On

1. Did you recognize yourself in any of the women I characterized above? Are you placing too much emphasis on one certain area of your life? If so, which one?

_____

_____

_____

_____

_____

2. Take a look at your life and rate yourself. What is the number one area of emphasis (the one you focus on most) for you? Number two? Number three? As you think about these areas, you know that you may need to concentrate on scaling back your endeavors in your number one area, while strengthening yourself in the others.

> *Not maintaining balance is like dissing yourself— and I know you don't want to do that.*

_____

_____

_____

_____

_____

3. What adjustments can you make in order to slowly but surely bring your body, mind, and spirit into balance?

_____

_____

_____

_____

_____

_____

Learn Your Lines

So God created man in His own image; in the image of God He created him; male and female He created them.
Genesis 1:27

For You formed my inward parts; You covered me in my mother's womb. I will praise You for I am fearfully and wonderfully made; marvelous are Your works, and that my soul knows very well.
Psalm 139:13, 14

Now may the God of peace Himself sanctify you completely; and may your whole spirit, soul and body be preserved blameless at the coming of our Lord Jesus Christ.
1 Thessalonians 5:23

Act 2: The Seesaw Approach

Do you remember playing in the park as a child? In the park where I played were monkey bars, a slide, and maybe even a merry-go-round. All of those were fine with me, but what I liked best was the seesaw, probably the most challenging of all the playground equipment. Where one person could ascend the ladder of the slide and then sail down the slick surface all by herself, the seesaw required two people. Not only did a person need a partner for the seesaw, she also needed that partner to be approximately the same weight in order for the seesaw to rock back and forth properly. It just didn't work right if those who sat on it were not balanced, but everybody enjoyed the ride when the balance was right.

Life is like a seesaw, isn't it? In my case, when I realized my need for balance, I also recognized that the more I perceived in my life, the more I was also able to *see*. I could not *see* myself as organized and on the ball until I *saw* how much I did not have things together. I could not *see* myself taking care of my body until I *saw* how out of shape I was and how desperately my eating habits needed to change.

When two children who are not close to the same size try to play on the seesaw, one will end up sitting on the ground all the time while the other will be up in the air. They have to see that their imbalance prohibits their ability to ride the seesaw together. Similarly, we have to recognize and admit when our lives are out of balance and are not operating as they should. Life really doesn't work if things are not balanced and if we do not put equal weight on body, mind, and spirit. When the emphasis on one is too heavy, everything else is left helplessly dan-

> *Everybody enjoys the ride when the balance is right.*

gling and stuck in mid-air. That lack of balance prevents the give-and-take that is necessary for success in life.

As I think about the whole issue of health and balance, I like to use a series of six instructions that will help you gain and maintain equilibrium in every area of your life. I call them "The Seesaw Approach." Each principle uses one of the letters of the word *seesaw*, and I've listed them for you below.

See yourself whole
Eat right and exercise
Expand your horizons
See the **S**pirit in everything
Shift your **A**ttitude
Be **W**ise

The next several chapters of this workbook are dedicated to these "seesaw" principles and will help you get established in them.

Life is like a seesaw, isn't it? It really doesn't work if things are not balanced and if we do not put equal weight on body, mind, and spirit.

You're On

1. As you look at the list of phrases that compose the seesaw approach, which one(s) do you need most in your life?

_____

_____

_____

_____

_____

2. As you look at the list of phrases that comprise the see-saw approach, which one(s) do you think you will find most challenging?

_____

_____

_____

_____

_____

3. If you look closely at the seesaw approach, you will quickly realize that it is not necessarily easy. It's healthy and it's good, but it isn't easy. Are you willing to climb on the see-saw and experiment with the various components of your life until the balance is right? Are you willing to commit to making the changes that are necessary in your life?

_____

_____

_____

_____

_____

_____

Learn Your Lines

Honest weights and scales are the Lord's;
all the weights in the bag are His work.
Proverbs 16:11

I have come that they may have life,
and that they may have it more abundantly.
John 10:10b

Therefore do not be unwise,
but understand what the will of the Lord is.
Ephesians 5:17

Beloved, I pray that you may prosper in all things
and be in health, just as your soul prospers.
3 John 2

COMING SOON

As you work to complete this workbook, please believe that change is possible for you. Yes, you. Perhaps for many years you have focused on one aspect of your life and neglected the others, but now is the perfect opportunity to begin to live differently. Would you use these pages to begin to dream about how your life would be if it were properly balanced? For instance, if you do not feel physically strong and in shape, what would you do if you were? If you have been neglecting yourself mentally, what would you like to learn? If you have let your spiritual life slide, what would you like to see happen in your relationship with God? Journal the good things you think can come from applying the seesaw approach to your life.

_____

_____

_____

_____

_____

_____

_____

ACTION!

Based on what you have learned in this chapter, what are three concise, measurable, attainable goals you will set for yourself when it comes to identifying areas that may be out of balance in your life and moving toward a more balanced way of living? You may want to list certain things to eliminate from your life or good habits to develop in the areas of your physical health, your mental health, or your spiritual health. Be sure to include a schedule and target date for reaching each goal and a reward for accomplishing it.

1. Goal: _____

Schedule and target completion date: _____

Reward: _____

_____

2. Goal: _____

Schedule and target completion date: _____

Reward: _____

_____

3. Goal: _____

Schedule and target completion date: _____

Reward: _____

_____

2

The Lady Sees Herself Whole

Introducing

want to make sure you know something — and not just that you know it, but that you believe it. *You are a whole person.* Yes, you are complete all by yourself. You don't need a man, a posh address, a prestigious job title, or cosmetic surgery to "fix" you or to fill in your gaps. Stop looking for other people to complete you; look for people with whom you can share your completeness. God made you to be one wonderful woman without anybody else's help. You are not broken; you are poised, capable, and confident. You are the kind of person people notice when you walk into a room. You are a leading lady, well on your way to that place of success and significance for which God created you.

You may want to say to me, "Dr. Cook, you don't even know me! How can you say that I am a confident woman? How can you say that heads turn when I walk into a room?" My sister, I don't have to know you to be sure of those things. Why? Because I know the God who made you, and I know the kind of work He does.

Now, you may have had some issues in your life — and your issues may have had issues! I'll give you some pointers to help you work through some of those. Nevertheless, you are designed to be whole, and God sees you whole through the blood of Jesus Christ. It's time to align your vision with God's and see yourself as the strong, healthy, whole woman He made you to be.

The Main Event

Act 1: Ponder Your Path

Proverbs 4:26 offers some excellent advice: "Ponder the path of your feet, and let all your ways be established." Do you know what it means to "ponder the path of your feet"? Quite simply, it means to think about where you are and where you are going. It means to take stock of your life and to take an honest look at yourself.

One of the first steps of the journey toward wholeness is to recognize where you may be broken and to acknowledge those situations that cause you pain. Isn't it true that if you want to see where you are going, you have to know where you are? Likewise, if you are going to see yourself whole, you first have to see where you are not whole. Your pain threatens your wholeness, but it also points you toward wholeness because it shows you where you need to be strengthened and healed. Once you see your pain, you can deal with it — and that will get you a long way down the road toward becoming whole.

> *I want to make sure you know something — and not just that you know it, but that you believe it.* **You are a whole person.**

As you begin to take an honest look at yourself, be aware that the best place to start is in a place of humility — total honesty before the Lord, a deep willingness to admit that some things are not as they should be in your life. Why humility? Because humility is the opposite of pride, and pride will prevent you from seeing what needs to be dealt with in your life. It is a tool of the enemy because he will do everything in his power to keep you from becoming healthy and whole. So humble yourself in the sight of the Lord and tell Him the whole truth about the way you've been living. Tell Him what's working, what isn't, where you need to forgive, where you need to improve, where you need to stop judging others. Go ahead and shoot straight with the good, the bad, and the ugly — all of those things that could make you say, "Ouch!" The good news is that it will move you toward healing and, as the Bible says in James 4:10, when you humble yourself, He will lift you up!

> *Stop looking for other people to complete you; look for people with whom you can share your completeness.*

You're On

1. When was the last time you "pondered the path of your feet"? Doesn't now seem like a good time to do that (or to do it again)?

_____

_____

_____

_____

_____

_____

_____

2. What is the most significant challenge to wholeness in your life? Or what has prevented you from feeling whole? A broken relationship? Having been abused? Lack of education you feel you need? Some sort of failure you can't seem to overcome? Feelings of worthlessness?

Ponder the path of your feet, and let all your ways be established.

Proverbs 4:26

_____

_____

_____

_____

_____

3. Are you willing to humble yourself before the Lord and take an honest look at yourself? What are the areas of your life where you struggle the most to be honest and humble? Would you write those down in the space below? As you do, determine that you will not let them slide and you will deal with them.

_____

_____

_____

_____

_____

_____

_____

_____

_____

> *If you are going to see yourself whole, you first have to see where you are not whole.*

Learn Your Lines

*When my heart is overwhelmed; lead me
to the rock that is higher than I.*

Psalm 61:2b

*Trust in the Lord with all your heart, and lean not on your
own understanding; in all your ways acknowledge Him, and
He shall direct your paths.*

Proverbs 3:5, 6

*Therefore, humble yourselves under the mighty hand of God,
that He may exalt you in due time, casting all your care on
Him, for He cares for you.*

1 Peter 5:6, 7

Act 2: On Your Way to Wholeness

There is not a quick and easy formula for healing when
we walk with the Lord, and no one can heal you or go
through the healing process for you. Thank God for the
Holy Spirit! He is our Helper and our Comforter and the
Healer of broken hearts. He can be very creative and personal as He mends our hearts. I can encourage you and I can
cheer you on, but I can't do it for you. However, I can offer
you some general suggestions that I believe will help you,
listed below. Be brutally honest, and go through this exercise as many times as necessary. Remember that wholeness
is a process and that often, the Holy Spirit will take you
through seasons of healing and wholeness, so expect to need

to do this again as He brings certain events or circumstances to your mind in the days to come.

◆ Now, I really want you to be healed and whole, so I trust you to get alone in the presence of the Lord and let the healing begin.

◆ Think about the painful times and situations in your life. Do they still hurt?

◆ In your own words, give your pain to the Lord. Tell Him that you release it. If you need to repent because you responded to your situation in an ungodly way, ask Him to forgive you.

◆ Ask the Holy Spirit to heal your heart and to minister His wholeness in that aspect of your life.

◆ Ask the Holy Spirit to help you see yourself whole. Thank and praise Him for doing that!

◆ Find scriptures that will help strengthen you as you begin to walk in wholeness in this area. Meditate on them, pray them, and thank God for the truth of His Word.

◆ Ask the Holy Spirit to remind you of other situations that have caused you to be broken and repeat these steps as you need to.

Because this issue of healing is so critical to your wholeness, I want to make sure you have everything you need in order to fully receive the grace and healing God has for you, and offer you an example of the pattern I have laid before you.

◆ A woman remembers a break-up or a divorce or a broken relationship with a friend. The memory is still painful and she still feels the hurt of rejection.

◆ The woman says to the Lord, "Father, this still hurts. But I don't want to cling to the pain anymore. I release it to You in Jesus' name. I am so sorry that I did not respond in love to those who rejected me and I ask You to forgive me. . .

◆ She continues: "Holy Spirit, I ask You to heal my heart and minister Your wholeness to this broken place in me. I thank You that You are healing me and strengthening me!

◆ She gets out her Bible and looks for scriptures that will combat those old feelings of rejection, scriptures that remind her how much God loves her and how thoroughly He accepts her. She finds verses such as Jeremiah 31:3, which says, "The Lord has appeared of old to me saying: 'Yes, I have loved you with an everlasting love; Therefore with lovingkindness I have drawn you.'" She memorizes the verse and rehearses it in her mind often. She prays it, saying something like "Father, I thank You for the truth of Your Word and I thank You that You love me with an everlasting love. Thank You for accepting me and drawing me to Yourself with lovingkindness . . ."

> *Thank God for the Holy Spirit! He is our Helper and our Comforter and the Healer of broken hearts.*

◆ When she feels a release from the current situation, she asks the Holy Spirit to take her through this kind of healing process again in His time and in His way.

You're On

1. What past experience or present situation in your life would benefit from this healing process?

_____

_____

_____

_____

_____

_____

Remember that wholeness is a process and that often the Holy Spirit will take you through seasons of healing and wholeness.

2. Do you need to ask forgiveness for any way that you responded to that situation or past experience?

_____

_____

_____

_____

_____

_____

_____

3. What scriptures can you find to help you as you allow the Holy Spirit to heal you?

_____

_____

_____

_____

_____

_____

_____

Learn Your Lines

You will show me the path of life; In Your presence is fullness of joy; At Your right hand are pleasures forevermore.

Psalm 16:11

I will instruct you and teach you in the way you should go; I will guide you with My eye.

Psalm 32:8

"Come, and let us go up to the mountain of the Lord, to the house of the God of Jacob; He will teach us His ways, and we shall walk in His paths."

Micah 4:2

COMING SOON

*W*ould you do something for me? Begin to see yourself whole. Right now, begin to see yourself as a complete woman — strong and healthy and balanced. Can you see her? Now, take your pen and write about this woman. Don't forget; she is you. What do you see when you see yourself whole?

_____

_____

_____

_____

_____

_____

_____

_____

_____

_____

_____

_____

ACTION!

*B*ased on what you have learned in this chapter, what are three concise, measurable, attainable goals you will set for yourself when it comes to being honest about where you are right now, moving toward personal wholeness and seeing yourself whole? Be sure to include a schedule and target date for reaching each goal and a reward for accomplishing it.

1. Goal: _____

Schedule and target completion date: _____

Reward: _____

_____

2. Goal: _____

Schedule and target completion date: _____

Reward: _____

_____

3. Goal: _____

Schedule and target completion date: _____

Reward: _____

_____

3

The Lady Eats Right

Introducing

o you ever walk down the aisle at your church and think something or someone is following you — and it's you? If your history or culture is anything like mine, most of your meals normally included fatback and ham hock. We put salt on everything — potatoes, tomatoes, even watermelon! Listen to me, Sister — that stuff can mess us up! In 1 Corinthians 6:19, God claims our bodies as holy dwelling places for His Spirit. Our "temples" need to glorify God, but I see an awful lot of women who are overweight and who do not seem to eat healthily. If you are going to be a leading lady, you need to be physically healthy and to make sure you are feeding your body well. I hope this chapter will help you get off to a good start so that you'll be in shape — spirit, mind, and body — when you step into the spotlight on center stage.

Act 1: Your Diet and Nutrition

The United States is a fat nation. The latest statistics from the National Health and Nutrition Examination Survey show that

◆ 64.5% of American adults — more than 120 million people — are overweight or obese (and it's carrying over to our children. America has the most obese children in the world)

◆ 31% of those adults are obese, which means that they are 30 pounds or more above healthy body weight

◆ there are more obese women (33%) than men (28%)

◆ between 55 and 65.8% of all African American women in the United States are overweight or obese

◆ while only 5% of all obese adults are considered "extremely obese," 15% of black women are in this category

◆ there are more obese African American women than any other race of woman, overwhelmingly

If you are not a part of either the obese or the overweight categories, congratulations — you've beaten the odds! But there is a chance that you are either overweight or obese, which means these statistics should concern you. *Obesity* is defined as being 30 or more pounds over a healthy body weight and, for women, this means you possess more than 30% body fat. *Overweight*, on the other hand, refers to a total body weight (including fat, bone and muscle) that is 10 to 30 pounds over a healthy body weight. The standard for determining if you're overweight or obese is body mass index (BMI), which measures a person's weight in relation to his or her height. To calculate your BMI, divide your weight (in kilograms) by your height (in meters) squared (1 Kilogram=2.2 lbs.). A BMI rating of 25 or more is considered overweight, while 30 or more is obese.

The more overweight you are, the greater your risk for developing diabetes, heart disease, liver disease, various cancers, high blood pressure, stroke, arthritis, and many other health problems. Simply put, this could be a life or death issue for you.

Whatever the reasons are for this serious condition, it does stress the necessity for change in three areas of your habits: diet, exercise, and nutrition. Note the difference between a change in diet and *dieting*. Dieting is temporarily abstaining from certain foods to reach a targeted weight loss. Most women who diet find themselves on an emotional roller coaster that fluctuates as often as their actual weight. As helpful as some fad diets can be, they cannot replace a true lifestyle change in diet. And for most women, this lifestyle change begins with a new approach to eating habits.

> *To calculate your BMI, divide your weight (in kilograms) by your height (in meters) squared.*

Ladies, please read this carefully: You should always consult your physician before starting any exercise program and before making any drastic changes to your diet or nutrition program. You may have some physical issues that would be adversely affected by such changes. Checking with your doctor first and getting his or her advice will help you to better accomplish your health goals.

You're On

1. Do you treat your body as a temple of the Holy Spirit? Does it honor and glorify God?

_____

_____

_____

_____

_____

_____

The more overweight you are, the greater risk you have for developing diabetes, heart disease, liver disease, various cancers, high blood pressure, stroke, arthritis, and many other health problems.

2. Are you overweight or obese? If so, how does that make you feel?

_____

_____

_____

_____

_____

_____

_____

3. When it comes to diet and nutrition, what lifestyle changes can you begin to make now?

_____

_____

_____

_____

_____

Learn Your Lines

But He answered and said, "It is written: 'Man shall not live by bread alone, but by every word that proceeds from the mouth of God.'"

Matthew 4:4

All things are lawful for me, but all things are not helpful. All things are lawful for me, but I will not be brought under the power of any.

1 Corinthians 6:12

Do you not know that your body is the temple of the Holy Spirit who is in you, whom you have from God, and you are not your own? For you were bought at a price; therefore glorify God in your body and in your spirit, which are God's.

1 Corinthians 6:19, 20

Therefore, whether you eat or drink,
or whatever you do, do all to the glory of God.
1 Corinthians 10:31

Act 2: Making Healthy Changes

The primary change needed in many women's diets is a radical reduction in fat allowance. The total fat in your diet should comprise no more than 30% of your total calories, with saturated fats making up for no more than 10% of that. Too much saturated fat raises the amount of cholesterol in your blood, which in turn can clog your arteries and increase your risk of heart disease. Here are some high-fat foods to avoid:

◆ whole or 2% milk

◆ sausage, bacon, veal, or pork

◆ butter and margarine

◆ carbohydrates

◆ shortening

◆ cheeses

◆ donuts, sweet rolls, or muffins

◆ whole sour cream

◆ fried foods

◆ "dark meat" turkey and chicken

(This list is repeated in Appendix B so that you can cut it out and put it on your refrigerator or somewhere else where it can serve as a reminder to you).

To replace the items listed above in your diet, choose low-fat or lean items. Opt for skim and low fat in all dairy products. When selecting meats, choose lean ones such as turkey or chicken breasts. Lean beef and veal cuts have the word *loin* or *round* in their names; lean pork cuts have the word *loin* or *leg* in their names. But here's a tip: Don't always trust the "low-fat" label that's become a hallmark for marketing food. Check out the actual fat gram count and remember to consider this in relation to the actual serving size.

As you change your fat allowance, also keep an eye on your calorie allowance. Your total calorie intake depends on your weight and height. If you're not aware of how many calories you should be consuming each day, ask your doctor.

The formula is simple, however: To lose weight, you must expend more calories than you consume. As a result of watching your calorie consumption, it's crucial to develop healthy eating portions. Unlike the small breakfast, big lunch, even-bigger dinner approach that most busy Americans take, the healthiest way to eat is to consume five to six meals a day in significantly smaller portions and increase your exercise.

A correct portion size is approximately the size of your fist, and each meal includes two to three portions. I recommend that you always start your morning with a hearty breakfast — eggs, yogurt, and a piece of fruit make for a great beginning to your busy day. It's important to know that eggs are high in cholesterol, so limit eggs to 2 a week, unless you get rid of the yolks or use an egg substitute like Egg Beaters®.

Snacks between meals can be fruits, vegetables, or a low-sugar health bar. A mid-day grilled chicken salad can hit the spot, while a dinner including salmon, fresh green beans, and a potato is a great way to end the day. Avoid eating after 8 p.m. and make sure all your snacks are low in sodium.

One key to eating right is eating natural, which means cutting out synthetic sugars found in most desserts, baked goods, processed snacks, and candies. Foods high in sugar tend to have empty calories — calories without other nutrients. Replace these with vegetables and fruits, which are low in fat and also contain fiber, vitamins, and minerals. Whole-grain products are also low in fat and high in fiber. Build meals around these healthy foods and go easier on dairy and meat products. Once again, avoid foods high in sodium, and minimize your use of salt in cooking. Your daily salt intake should be no more than 6 grams (1 teaspoon).

At the foundation of both effective weight loss and healthy eating is one thing: water. Water is instrumental in regulating body temperature, maintaining blood volume, and eliminating waste. It can also act as an appetite suppressant. Your daily intake of water should be eight 8-ounce glasses of water. Try drinking 12 to 16 ounces of water before each meal to help satisfy your hunger. At every opportunity, drink water rather than a carbonated beverage. To help you, carry a large water bottle with you to sip on throughout the day. And for additional flavor, try adding a lemon or lime. I always start each day with a big glass of ice water and I sip water throughout the day.

If flavor continues to be a concern as you cook healthier meals for you and your family, know that there are alterna-

Don't always trust the "low-fat" label that's become a hallmark for marketing food. Check out the actual fat gram count and remember to consider this in relation to the actual serving size.

tives to the old, fat-abundant ways you may have prepared meals. In Appendix B, you will find some specific suggestions to help you cook healthily.

Finally, as you continue to change your eating habits toward a healthier diet, make sure you are getting the proper nutrients either through natural foods or through dietary supplements (vitamins). Don't forego healthy eating simply because you've begun taking a dietary supplement. There is no replacing a healthy, balanced diet with daily portions of fruits, vegetables, whole grains, low-fat dairy, poultry, and fish — all of which should provide sufficient vitamins and minerals for your body. However, if dietary supplementation is necessary for you, look for multivitamins that contain at least 100% of the following vitamins: A, B-1 (thiamin), B-2 (riboflavin), B-6, B-12, C, D, E, folic acid, and niacin. Women 25 years and older should also consider taking calcium (at least 800 milligrams) and iron (at least 15 milligrams) supplements.

When you decide to lose weight, remember that the healthy approach is gradual. While fad diets promise dramatic results within six weeks, the outcome is temporary and can actually be detrimental in the long run. The key is a lifestyle change. If you're committed to losing weight the healthy way, aim for losing up to a pound each week. If you're overweight, losing as little as 5 to 10% of your body weight might improve many of the health problems linked to being overweight. And if your goal is simply to have a healthier diet, you'll quickly realize the drastic benefits of eating right.

Unlike the small breakfast, big lunch, even-bigger dinner approach most busy Americans take, the healthiest way to eat is to consume five to six meals a day in significantly smaller portions (fist-sized portions).

You're On

1. What high-fat foods do you need to eliminate from your diet?

_____

_____

_____

_____

_____

_____

If your goal is to lose weight, remember that the healthy approach is gradual. The key is a lifestyle change. If you're committed to losing weight the healthy way, aim for losing up to a pound each week.

2. If you are truly going to change your lifestyle, what changes do you need to make in the way you cook?

_____

_____

_____

_____

_____

_____

_____

3. Are you getting enough nutrients? If not, are you taking your vitamins? (If you aren't, now is a great time to start!)

_____

_____

_____

_____

_____

_____

_____

Learn Your Lines

*Have you found honey? Eat only as much as you need,
lest you be filled with it and vomit.*
Proverbs 25:16

*Remove falsehood and lies far from me; give me neither poverty
nor riches — feed me with the food allotted to me.*
Proverbs 30:8

*I know that nothing is better than for them to rejoice,
and do good in their lives, and also that every man
should eat and drink and enjoy the good of all his labor —
it is the gift of God.*
Ecclesiastes 3:12, 13

COMING SOON

When you think about eating right and knowing that you are taking good care of yourself nutritionally, what physical changes do you hope to see? How do you expect to feel different emotionally? (I'll tell you a secret — eating right and treating your body well is extremely empowering)! What do you look forward to doing or being able to do that you can't do now?

ACTION!

*B*ased on what you have learned in this chapter, what are three concise, measurable, attainable goals you will set for yourself in the area of good nutrition and eating right? Be sure to include a schedule and target date for reaching each goal and a reward for accomplishing it.

1. Goal: _____

Schedule and target completion date: _____

Reward: _____

_____

2. Goal: _____

Schedule and target completion date: _____

Reward: _____

_____

3. Goal: _____

Schedule and target completion date: _____

Reward: _____

_____

4

The Lady Exercises Regularly

Introducing

Even leading ladies battle the temptation to compare themselves physically with other women. No matter how beautiful everyone says you are, you may be like so many women — always on the lookout to see whose waist is smaller and whose thighs are tighter! Yet in all the comparing and measuring up to the ideal, one thing remains true: God created your body. The same body you may find disgusting is the one He cherishes; the body you may avoid looking at in the mirror is the same one He has His eye on constantly. So before we think any more about health, fitness or weight loss, understand this: God loves you as you are.

By the same token, His Word challenges us to present our bodies as a "living sacrifice." Sacrifices aren't haphazardly thrown on the altar; they're meticulously prepared. Hours, even days, are spent worrying if every detail of the sacrifice will find approval. For the one who prepares the sacrifice, there is a single focus: the acceptance and pleasure of the One to whom the sacrifice is offered.

Likewise, our bodies are sacrifices to God, meaning that we should constantly be preparing them for His delight. Even if your dress size or body measurements do not meet the world's ideals, you can be confident in knowing His pleasure when you've done all you can to prepare yourself as a living sacrifice. This means keeping our bodies fit. Most Christians wholeheartedly believe that the Scripture states our bodies are temples for the Holy Spirit (see 1 Cor. 6:19), but some forget the words of Ecclesiastes 10:18: "because of laziness the building decays." When we get lazy and allow our bodies to become physically inactive, we invite disease, sickness, and physical deterioration. If we keep our bodies fit, however, we strengthen every part and honor God's command.

Today, discover how you can worship God with your body and be physically fit and strong enough to fulfill all the demands of your role as a leading lady.

The Main Event

Act 1: A Living Sacrifice

Despite the supposed "health craze" that has swept across the United States within the past decade, more than 70% of all adults in this country still aren't involved in the recommended amount of regular physical activity. The Centers for Disease Control and Prevention defines 30 minutes of moderate-intensity physical activity for at least five days each week as a recommended amount. In every age category, women are less active than men, and African American women between the ages of 25 and 34 are more likely to gain weight than any other segment of the population. Whatever race you are a member of, I want you to understand this now so that you can take action because the older you get, the less likely you are to exercise enough.

If hearing these grim facts creates a resolve in you to defy the odds, there's good news: Getting fit isn't difficult. Your model of a healthy woman doesn't have to be a thick-necked, iron-pumping hunk of a woman who lifts weights for a living, nor does it have to be the paper-thin, perfectly toned model on the magazine cover. Your level of fitness is uniquely you. All it takes is the determination to get your body in the best physical shape it can be. But be forewarned: Most people who set out to get in shape start strong, but give up within a few weeks. The key is to start with realistic goals and to not jump into getting fit with too much zeal and not enough perseverance. Pace yourself. And on days you feel like relaxing and skipping another workout, remind yourself of the following benefits to exercising. Staying fit

In every age category, women are less active than men, and African American women between the ages of 25 and 34 are more likely to gain weight than any other segment of the population.

- reduces the risk of dying prematurely

- reduces the risk of stroke

- reduces the risk of developing and/or dying from coronary heart disease

- reduces the risk of having a second heart attack if you've already had a heart attack

- reduces the risk of developing Type 2 diabetes

◆ reduces total blood cholesterol and increases high-density lipoproteins (the "good" cholesterol)

◆ reduces the risk of developing high blood pressure and helps reduce blood pressure if you already have hypertension

◆ reduces the risk of developing colon cancer

◆ reduces feelings of depression and anxiety

◆ helps control weight, builds lean muscle, and reduces fat

◆ helps build and maintain healthy bones, muscles, and joints

◆ helps older adults become stronger and better able to move without falling

◆ promotes psychological well-being and reduces stress

> *Most people who set out to get in shape start strong but give up within a few weeks. The key is to start with realistic goals. Too much zeal at first can hurt your long term perseverance.*

You're On

1. Do you include a fitness routine in your daily or weekly activities? If not, why?

_____

_____

_____

_____

_____

2. If you are not exercising regularly, how can you change your schedule to include exercising?

_____

_____

_____

_____

_____

_____

3. What activity or activities do you need to start in order to begin or improve your fitness routine?

_____

_____

_____

_____

_____

_____

_____

Learn Your Lines

*I beseech you therefore, brethren, by the mercies of God,
that you present your bodies a living sacrifice, holy, acceptable
to God, which is your reasonable service.*

Romans 12:1

*Or do you not know that your body is the temple of the
Holy Spirit who is in you, whom you have from God,
and you are not your own?*

1 Corinthians 6:19

*[We are] always carrying about in the body the dying
of the Lord Jesus, that the life of Jesus may also
be manifested in our body.*

2 Corinthians 4:10

Act 2: On Your Mark, Get Set

We all know remaining physically inactive can result in weight gain. But did you also know the other health risks you create by not exercising? Heart disease, diabetes, depression, obesity, colon cancer, high blood pressure. . . these are just a few of the conditions you could develop by not keeping fit. The bottom line is that your body needs exercise to stay healthy. No matter what health obstacle you're facing — whether you're 100 pounds overweight or you're recovering from breast cancer — you can be a healthy, fit woman.

Before launching into your newly inspired workout regimen, the most important thing to do is to consult a doctor. Most people bypass this crucial step toward healthiness, assuming they know everything that's going on with their body, inside and out. The truth is, your doctor can detect situations and conditions that you can't. Before starting any kind of exercise program, have a thorough physical examination. Besides the need to know of any medical conditions that may affect your fitness plans, it's crucial to get an assessment of your heart condition. More than any other muscle, your heart is at the core of all exercise. To lose weight, build muscle, or simply improve your health, your heart rate should remain within its targeted or training zone while you exercise. Ask your doctor what this is for you. Also check with your doctor about any medications you're currently on, and make sure these will not put you at risk while exercising. If you currently have a health condition such as diabetes or heart disease, consulting with your doctor is a must.

The key is to do one of two things: Either engage in a moderate-intensity activity for at least 30 minutes for five or more days each week, or engage in a vigorous-intensity activity for at least 20 minutes for three or more days each week.

Once you're cleared to begin your fitness program, remember to start small. One of the most common (and most detrimental) mistakes among those trying to get back into shape is initially overworking their bodies. If you haven't jogged in five years, don't expect to run a mile in six minutes. If you haven't taken a swim since you were a teenager, don't bolt into a 50-lap freestyle routine. Your body must be prepped for increased activity — gradually.

One of the best ways to do this, and to avoid soreness or injury, is by stretching for at least 10 minutes both before and after your activity. Stretching does just that — it stretches your muscles, allowing you to increase your range of motion while also stimulating muscle growth. After you've exercised, stretching again can help to get rid of lactic acid from muscle tissue, which can otherwise cause cramps and soreness.

Determining which physical activity is best for you is like choosing which car fits your personality; it's completely up to you. One of the exciting aspects of getting fit is the hundreds of ways you can work your body into shape without ever falling into a boring routine. Choose an activity you'll enjoy. If you're competitive in nature, try an individual or team sport such as tennis or basketball. If you desire an activity that also gives you time to think, try walking, jogging, or swimming. I do a combination of walking, swimming, and a team sport. Even though it may seem tiring at first, it becomes exhilarating and adds energy to your day. The key is to do one of two things: Either engage in a moderate-intensity activity for at least 30 minutes for five or more days each week, or engage in a vigorous-intensity activity for at least 20 minutes for three or more days each week.

A moderate amount of physical activity is roughly equivalent to physical activity that uses approximately 150 calories of energy per day. Moderate-intensity activities are ones in which you are exerting energy yet can comfortably continue a conversation. For example, moderate-intensity activities could include

> *A well-balanced weight-training routine can improve your joints, bones, muscles, organs and immune system. Increasing muscle mass allows the body to burn more calories, which in turn helps you lose weight.*

- Washing and waxing a car for 45 to 60 minutes

- Washing windows or floors for 45 to 60 minutes

- Gardening for 30 to 45 minutes

- Basketball (shooting baskets) for 30 minutes

- Wheeling self in wheelchair for 30 to 40 minutes

- Swimming laps for 20 minutes

- Walking 2 miles in 35 minutes (20 min/mile)

- Raking leaves for 30 minutes

- Shoveling snow for 15 minutes

- Stair walking for 15 minutes

A vigorous-intensity activity involves more energy and could include activities such as:

- Bicycling 4 miles on rugged terrain in 15 minutes

- Basketball (game) for 10 to 15 minutes

- Running 1 mile in 12 minutes

- Aerobic dancing for 30 minutes

As you ease into a fitness program, gradually increase your exercise time and intensity. All of these exercises are particularly effective in helping you lose weight. While any exercise is good to begin your fitness program, you may eventually want to begin strength training or weight training. While some women shy away from lifting weights for fear of bulking up, the average woman doesn't come close to lifting the weight amounts necessary to create that kind of body. In truth, a well-balanced weight training routine can improve your joints, bones, muscles, organs, and immune system. Increasing muscle mass allows the body to burn more calories, which in turn helps you lose weight. I began my fitness program two years ago and have seen and felt a noticeable difference in my body, the fit of my clothes, my overall health, and self esteem.

Whatever exercises you engage in on your way to becoming healthier, realize that fitness doesn't just involve activities — it's a lifestyle change. For most of us, finding time in our hectic schedules for exercise is a challenge. The good news is that exercise can be incorporated into any schedule, no matter how busy. Here are some easy and practical ways to squeeze in exercise throughout the day:

◆ Walk, cycle, or jog to work, school, the store, or church.

◆ Park the car a few blocks away from your destination and walk.

◆ Take the stairs instead of the elevator or escalator.

◆ If you can't find 30 minutes to do your activity at one time, break it up into 10-minute segments.

◆ Play with children or pets. Everybody wins.

◆ During breaks at work, walk around the block/office or do desk exercises. (Be prepared by keeping a pair of comfortable walking or running shoes in your car or office).

◆ Avoid labor-saving devices (i.e. turn off the self-propel option on your lawn mower or vacuum cleaner).

◆ Exercise while watching TV (i.e. use hand weights, stationary bicycle/treadmill/stair climber or stretch).

◆ Make a Saturday morning with your girlfriends a group exercise habit.

◆ Walk while doing errands.

You're On

1. What are some of the health risks associated with failure to exercise?

_____

_____

_____

_____

_____

_____

_____

_____

_____

_____

2. What is the most important thing you can do before beginning a fitness routine or an exercise regimen?

_____

_____

_____

_____

_____

_____

3. Of the suggestions offered in the lists above, what can you do to increase your level of physical activity?

_____

_____

_____

_____

_____

_____

_____

Learn Your Lines

*Give attention to My words; incline your ear
to my sayings. Do not let them depart from your eyes;
keep them in the midst of your heart; for they are life
to those who find them, and health to all their flesh.*

Proverbs 4:20-22

*The Lord will guide you continually and satisfy
your soul in drought, and strengthen your bones;
you shall be like a well-watered garden, like a spring
of water, whose waters do not fail.*

Isaiah 58:11

*Therefore, do not let sin reign in your mortal body,
that you should obey it in its lusts.*

Romans 6:12

*Therefore strengthen the hands which hang down,
and the feeble knees, and make straight paths for your feet,
so that what is lame may not be dislocated,
but rather be healed.*

Hebrews 12:12

COMING SOON

*C*an you imagine how you will feel when you are stronger and fit? What will it be like to carry around fewer pounds and to have a trimmer waistline? What will you do with increased strength — play with your children or grandchildren more, buy a new outfit, hike a nature trail? Whatever it is that you look forward to, take a few minutes and dream on paper about the time you will be able to experience your goal.

ACTION!

*B*ased on what you have learned in this chapter, what are three concise, measurable, attainable goals you will set for yourself in the area of exercise and fitness? Be sure to include a schedule and target date for reaching each goal and a reward for accomplishing it.

1. Goal: _____

Schedule and target completion date: _____

Reward: _____

_____

2. Goal: _____

Schedule and target completion date: _____

Reward: _____

_____

3. Goal: _____

Schedule and target completion date: _____

Reward: _____

_____

5

The Lady Expands Her Horizons

Introducing

f you are going to live a balanced life as a leading lady, I encourage you to expand your horizons. Sometimes, we get so busy, as women, just trying to do everything we need to do and take care of everyone else that we fail to try new things. It's easy to get stuck in the ruts of our personal routines, but there is more to life than what goes on in your church or at your workplace or in your family or in your neighborhood. There are so many ways to stimulate your mind, to jumpstart your body on a physical fitness routine, and to experience fresh power and intimacy in your spiritual life — and I'll give you some great ideas in this chapter. I urge you to start looking for more in every area of your life.

You may have heard the phrase, "Think outside the box." But leading ladies don't just *think* outside the box; they *get* outside the box! They take the risk, make the leap, and find themselves invigorated by new challenges and pursuits. So get ready; here we go!

The Main Event

Act 1: Be a Whopper® Woman

I have a confession to make. I really do try to eat well and I don't eat much fast food, but when I do, I head straight for Burger King® and order up a Whopper® with everything on it. I want it dripping with ketchup, mayonnaise and mustard; I want it packed with pickles, onions, and tomatoes. I want absolutely everything they can possibly put on that burger. I am not a 99-cent-puny-burger-with-a-thin-little-patty-and-a-flimsy-bun-and-a-dab-of-ketchup kind of gal; I am Whopper® woman!

I have the same approach toward God. I'm saying, "Lord, give me everything You've got! Do not hold anything back. I want it all!" I tell Him, "Any way You want to bless me, I'll be satisfied." And do you know something? Every time I turn around, He's blessing me.

Are you the same way? Are you a Whopper® woman? Do you want everything God has for you? And are you willing to expand your horizons so that you can be a good steward of every blessing He wants to pour out in your life? Leading ladies live to the limit. They take full advantage of every opportunity and maximize every moment. They are committed to continually growing in every area of their lives — physically, mentally, and spiritually. They do not settle for less than God's best under any circumstances.

> *I do not want you to be a puny-burger lady; I want you to be a Whopper® woman!*

You're On

1. In what areas of your life are you settling for less than God's very best?

_____

_____

_____

_____

_____

_____

_____

2. What do you need to do in order to improve in the areas you listed above?

_____

_____

_____

_____

_____

_____

Leading ladies don't just think outside the box; they get outside the box!

3. What is the risk you would take if you knew you would not fail?

_____

_____

_____

_____

_____

_____

> *Leading ladies live to the limit.*

Learn Your Lines

And Jabez called on the God of Israel saying,
"Oh, that You would bless me indeed, and enlarge my territory,
that Your hand would be with me, and that You would
keep me from evil, that I may not cause pain!"
So God granted him what he requested.

1 Chronicles 4:10

May the Lord give you increase more and more,
you and your children.

Psalm 115:14

Enlarge the place of your tent, and let them stretch
out the curtains of your dwellings; do not spare;
lengthen your cords, and strengthen your stakes.
For you shall expand to the right and to the left . . .

Isaiah 54:2, 3

Act 2: Practical Ways to Expand Your Horizons

When I write about expanding your horizons, I can see many practical ways you could do it. For instance, develop new skills and interests; increase your knowledge in a subject you find fascinating; work on your physical strength; go on a spiritual retreat; or make a new friend. There are all sorts of ways to broaden the scope of your life experiences. To help you get started, I have listed below 10 or more suggestions in each of our three categories (body, mind, and spirit). I hope you'll start soon by incorporating some of these recommendations or coming up with some of your own.

Physically

Remember to check with your physician before starting any fitness routine or making significant nutritional changes.

1. Join a health club.

2. Invest in some sessions with a personal trainer.

3. Buy some small weights and lift them while watching the news.

4. Take the stairs instead of the elevator.

5. Drink water instead of caffeinated beverages.

6. Cut down on red meat and eat more fruits and vegetables.

7. Take your vitamins.

> *There are many ways to stimulate your mind, to jumpstart your body on a physical fitness routine, and to experience fresh power and intimacy in your spiritual life.*

8. Get enough rest.

9. With appropriate instruction and supervision, do something you've never done before, but always thought you'd enjoy — like mountain biking, horseback riding, ice-skating, or racquetball.

10. Walk a predetermined course or distance every day or several times a week.

11. When you're on the road, visit your hotel's fitness center. Often they have personal trainers available.

12. Take a swim.

Mentally

1. Read the newspaper.

2. Keep up with current events through a weekly news magazine or through television.

3. Attend a lecture at your local college or university.

4. Subscribe to a trade journal or magazine that focuses on your profession.

5. Join a professional or civic association.

6. Set a reading goal — a book per week, a book per month, whatever works for you.

7. Attend a conference or seminar pertaining to your career or area of interest.

8. Take a course at your local high school or community college.

9. Take advantage of the resources available at your local library.

10. If you do not have a high school diploma, work on your GED. If you have always longed to finish college or get a graduate degree, go for it!

11. If you are "shy" about your public speaking, join a local "Toastmasters."

12. Find a personal "coach" like myself, who you can hire to work with you.

Spiritually

1. Find a prayer partner — share your needs and pray for one another.

2. Make sure you are reading the Bible daily and letting it get into your heart, not just your mind.

3. Go to church — and really worship.

4. Fast.

5. Be thankful; thanksgiving turns your heart toward the Lord.

6. Stay clean — don't let sin fester in your heart.

7. Stay humble — remember that God gives grace to the humble.

8. Take a private prayer retreat, even if it is just for an afternoon or for one day.

9. Fill your home and your car with worship music — and sing along.

> *Develop new skills and interests; increase your knowledge in a subject you find fascinating; work on your physical strength; go on a spiritual retreat; or make a new friend.*

10. Use a daily devotional book and set aside a few quiet moments each day to read it. May I suggest:

> *Sister to Sister: Devotions for African American Women* by Suzan Johnson Cook
>
> *Woman, Thou Art Loosed Devotional* by T. D. Jakes
>
> *Sister Wit* by Jacqueline Jakes
>
> *My Utmost for His Highest* by Oswald Chambers
>
> *Streams in the Desert* by L. B. Cowman
>
> *Too Blessed to Be Stressed* by Suzan Johnson Cook

You're On

1. What have you always wanted to learn about, but have not?

_____

_____

_____

_____

_____

_____

_____

2. What sport or activity have you always wanted to try, but haven't?

_____

_____

_____

_____

_____

_____

_____

_____

3. What do you long for in your relationship with the Lord, or what changes would you like to make in the way you live your spiritual life?

_____

_____

_____

_____

_____

_____

_____

_____

Learn Your Lines

I will run the course of Your commandments,
for You shall enlarge my heart.
Psalm 119:32

And do not be conformed to this world, but be transformed
by the renewing of your mind . . .
Romans 12:2

Be diligent to present yourself approved to God,
a worker who does not need to be ashamed,
rightly dividing the word of truth.
2 Timothy 2:15

But you, beloved, building yourselves up on
your most holy faith, praying in the Holy Spirit,
keep yourselves in the love of God, looking for the mercy
of our Lord Jesus Christ unto eternal life.
Jude 20, 21

COMING SOON

*I*sn't it exciting to think about expanding your horizons? I encourage you right now to think for a moment about how you can personally get more out of life. Look back at your answers to the questions in Act 1. What would your life look like if you were to integrate these goals into it?

ACTION!

*B*ased on what you have learned in this chapter, what are three concise, measurable, attainable goals you will set for yourself when it comes to expanding your horizons? Be sure to include a schedule and target date for reaching each goal and a reward for accomplishing it.

1. Goal: _____

Schedule and target completion date: _____

Reward: _____

_____

2. Goal: _____

Schedule and target completion date: _____

Reward: _____

_____

3. Goal: _____

Schedule and target completion date: _____

Reward: _____

_____

6

The Lady Sees the Spirit in Everything

Introducing

eading lady, may I shoot straight with you? No matter how gifted you are, no matter how smart or anointed or together you are, no matter how impressive your stock portfolio or how large your salary, no matter how fit or trim you are or how many degrees you've earned, there is no such thing as a self-made woman. God is always working in our lives, ordering our steps, and orchestrating our circumstances. If it had not been for the Lord — well, who knows what would have happened to me, and who knows what would have happened to you!

One way to stay grounded spiritually is to see the Spirit in everything, to continually remember that God is working on your behalf and for your good. For instance, let's say you were disappointed because you did not get a certain job you really wanted. Did you ever stop to think about how totally in control God is, or did you just feel sorry for yourself? Did it ever occur to you that maybe He knew that company would downsize or close in six months? Or, have you ever cried over a broken relationship, only to end up praising God later because you realized that He spared you from an unhealthy or abusive situation? Perhaps you have not encountered these specific situations, but reading about them may have reminded you of some other occasion when you knew God was watching out for you. Sister, the Holy Spirit has been hovering over your life and He is still there — leading you, guiding you, and directing you. You just have to look for Him!

The Main Event

Act 1: You Need Help!

As you well know, leading ladies have busy lives. Sometimes the needs and demands seem endless, and there are more things to do in a day than there are hours in which to do them. If your life is as packed as mine, you need help!

There is no such thing as a self-made woman.

Many times, we look first to natural resources for assistance. If you are a corporate CEO or a manager, you probably have an administrative assistant. If you are a teacher, you may have an aide. If you are a doctor, you have a nurse. If you are an attorney, you have a paralegal. If you are a stay-at-home mother, you may have someone to help with the household duties, and if not, then your children may have chores for which they are responsible. Whatever the situation, we can all use some help.

The Bible tells us that the Holy Spirit is our Helper. He is the Spirit of God — the One in whom all the love and goodness, the very heart of God, dwell and operate on earth.

One of His roles is to assist us in times of need and in areas of weakness. I tell you, there is no better Helper anywhere! He does not exist simply to help you pray more fervently, though He does; or to assist you in worship, though He does. He is also available to you moment-by-moment to help you with the practical aspects of your life — decisions on the job, social dilemmas, relationships with friends and family, making a major purchase, and anything else you think of. Not only does He help you, He does so with your best interest in mind, with everlasting unconditional love for you, with unending grace and mercy — and from the position of being able to see your entire life, knowing what you need (or don't need!) now in order to prepare you for the great things ahead.

> *Sister, the Holy Spirit has been hovering over your life and He is still there — leading you, guiding you, and directing you. You just have to look for Him!*

I really encourage you to cultivate an intimate relationship with your Helper, the Holy Spirit. You can begin to do this through prayer — talking to Him, thanking Him for His presence, and asking Him to help and guide you. You can also do this through Bible reading and study, asking Him to reveal Himself to you during your time in the Word. In Act 2 of this chapter, I'll help you get started.

You're On

1. What specific experience(s) can you remember in which God has helped you or rescued you or bailed you out? Did you recognize that as the ministry of the Holy Spirit?

_____

_____

_____

_____

_____

_____

_____

The Holy Spirit is available to you moment-by-moment to help you with the practical aspects of your life.

2. In what specific areas of your life do you need the help of the Holy Spirit right now?

_____

_____

_____

_____

_____

_____

_____

3. Are there any situations in your life where you may be resisting the help of the Holy Spirit? (In other words, are you being stubborn or rebellious?) If so, what are they? Will you ask the Lord's forgiveness now and invite the Holy Spirit to minister to you in those circumstances in a fresh, new way?

_____

_____

_____

_____

_____

_____

_____

_____

Learn Your Lines

"Not by might nor by power, but by My Spirit,"
says the LORD of hosts.

Zechariah 4:6

And I will pray the Father, and He will give you another
Helper, that He may abide with you forever — the Spirit of
truth, whom the world cannot receive, because it neither sees
Him nor knows Him; but you know Him, for He dwells with
you and will be in you.

John 14:16, 17

But the Helper, the Holy Spirit, whom the Father will send in
my name, He will teach you all things, and bring to your
remembrance all things that I said to you.

John 14:26

Likewise the Spirit also helps in our weaknesses. For we do not
know what we should pray for as we ought, but the Spirit
Himself makes intercession for us with groanings which
cannot be uttered.

Romans 8:26

Act 2: The Ministry of the Holy Spirit in Your Life

I'd like to help you understand the person and the activities of the Holy Spirit so that you will be able to fully receive, enjoy, and benefit from His ministry in your life. He is your Helper, but He is oh-so-much more than that! The Bible is full of references to the Holy Spirit, of words and phrases that tell us who He is. I'll list below some of His attributes and the roles He plays so that you can get better acquainted with Him and recognize His movement in your life. (Even if you have a vibrant relationship with the Holy Spirit and know these scriptures well, perhaps they will serve as a good reminder!)

◆ The Holy Spirit is good (Ps. 143:10).

◆ The Holy Spirit is the Spirit of wisdom and understanding, of counsel and might, and of knowledge and of the fear of the Lord (Is. 11:2).

◆ The Holy Spirit will lift up a standard against the enemy (Is. 59:19).

◆ The Holy Spirit will teach you what to say (Luke 12:12).

◆ The Holy Spirit gives life (John 6:63).

◆ The Holy Spirit will teach you and bring to you remembrance of the teaching of Jesus (John 14:26).

> *Not only does the Holy Spirit help you, He does so with your best interest in mind, with everlasting unconditional love for you, with unending grace and mercy — and from the position of being able to see your entire life, knowing what you need (or don't need!) now in order to prepare you for the great things ahead.*

- The Holy Spirit guides you into truth (John 16:13).

- The Holy Spirit gives power (Acts 1:8).

- The Holy Spirit pours out the love of God in your heart (Rom. 5:5).

- The Holy Spirit is life (see Rom. 8:10).

- The Holy Spirit gives life to your mortal body (Rom. 8:11).

- The Holy Spirit is the Spirit of adoption, causing you to know God as your Father (Rom. 8:15, 16).

- The Holy Spirit helps you in your weaknesses and prays for you (Rom. 8:26).

- The Holy Spirit causes you to abound in hope (Rom. 15:13).

- The Holy Spirit teaches you spiritual things (1 Cor. 2:13).

- The Holy Spirit causes you to declare that Jesus is Lord (1 Cor. 12:3).

- The Holy Spirit gives you spiritual gifts (1 Cor. 12:7-11).

- The Holy Spirit guarantees your inheritance (Eph. 1:13).

- The Holy Spirit gives life (2 Cor. 3:6).

- The Holy Spirit is God (2 Cor. 3:17).

- The Holy Spirit of the Lord brings freedom (2 Cor. 3:17).

- The Holy Spirit transforms you (2 Cor. 3:18).

- The Holy Spirit gives you access to the Father (Eph. 2:18).

- The Holy Spirit sanctifies you (2 Thess. 2:13).

- The Holy Spirit washes and renews you (Titus 3:5).

- The Holy Spirit is the Spirit of grace (Heb. 10:29).

- The Holy Spirit lives in you and always gives you more grace (James 4:5, 6).

- The Holy Spirit moves people to speak the words of the Lord (2 Peter 1:21).

- The Holy Spirit is truth (1 John 5:6).

You're On

1. Looking at the list above, what do you most need the Holy Spirit to be in your life?

_____

_____

_____

_____

_____

_____

_____

_____

_____

_____

2. Looking at the list above, what do you most need the Holy Spirit to do for you?

_____

_____

_____

_____

_____

_____

3. Thinking back over your life, which qualities and/or ministries of the Holy Spirit do you recognize? (Now would be a good time to thank Him!)

_____

_____

_____

_____

_____

_____

Learn Your Lines

The Spirit of the Lord is upon Me, because He has anointed Me to preach the gospel to the poor; He has sent Me to heal the brokenhearted, to proclaim liberty to the captives and recovery of sight to the blind, to set at liberty those who are oppressed; to proclaim the acceptable year of the Lord.

Luke 4:18, 19

If you then, being evil, know how to give good gifts to your children, how much more will your heavenly Father give the Holy Spirit to those who ask Him?

Luke 11:13

The grace of the Lord Jesus Christ, and the love of God, and the communion of the Holy Spirit be with you all. Amen.

2 Corinthians 13:14

I say then: Walk in the Spirit, and you shall not fulfill the lusts of the flesh. For the flesh lusts against the Spirit, and the Spirit against the flesh; and these are contrary to one another, so that you do not do the things that you wish.

Galatians 5:16, 17

But the fruit of the Spirit is love, joy, peace, longsuffering [or, patience], kindness, goodness, faithfulness, gentleness, self-control. Against such there is no law.

Galatians 5:22, 23

COMING SOON

A close and living relationship with the Holy Spirit will give you hope and passion and vision for your life. In this "Coming Soon," maybe you would like to ask the Holy Spirit to help you and to share His heart with you. You might ask Him how He sees you, what He wants to help you with, or what changes He wants to bring in your life. Use this space to write your impressions.

ACTION!

*B*ased on what you have learned in this chapter, what are three concise, measurable, attainable goals you will set for yourself in your relationship with the Holy Spirit? Be sure to include a schedule and target date for reaching each goal and a reward for accomplishing it.

1. Goal: _____

Schedule and target completion date: _____

Reward: _____

_____

2. Goal: _____

Schedule and target completion date: _____

Reward: _____

_____

3. Goal: _____

Schedule and target completion date: _____

Reward: _____

_____

7

The Lady Shifts Her Attitude

Introducing

omans 12:2 exhorts us, "And do not be conformed to this world, but be *transformed by the renewing of your mind*, that you may prove what is that good and acceptable and perfect will of God" (italics mine). What does that scripture really teach us? It teaches us that we are changed as we change our minds. We must learn to change the way we think. As you learn to develop and share your positive approach to life's situations, circumstances, relationships, and crises, others will be encouraged and you will be strengthened.

The Main Event

Act 1: Making the Shift

Leading ladies are strong enough to make significant changes in their attitudes and thought patterns, but disciplined enough and mature enough to realize that lasting change does not take place overnight. Making permanent, healthy changes is a process requiring a concerted effort over a period of time. This may be a challenge to you, but let me assure you, a new attitude is worth the work!

In order to develop an entire set of healthy attitudes, you first need to identify the bad attitudes that are currently operating in your life. Perhaps I can help you with a few indicators of a bad attitude.

◆ You know you've got a bad attitude when you dread seeing a certain person, a group of people, or when you dread starting a task or an assignment.

◆ You know you've got a bad attitude when you put off something that needs to be done because you don't want to do it.

◆ You know you've got a bad attitude when you exhibit rebellion of any kind.

◆ You know you've got a bad attitude when you manipulate someone else into doing something for which you are responsible.

◆ You know you've got a bad attitude when you gripe or murmur or complain.

Leading ladies are strong enough to make significant changes in their attitudes and thought patterns, but disciplined enough and mature enough to realize that lasting change does not take place overnight.

Once you've identified your bad attitudes (and you will have a chance to write them down as you answer the questions below!), it's time for an adjustment. You are the only person on earth who can change your attitude. Yep, this responsibility falls solely on you. One of the best ways to begin to shift your attitude is to first ask the Holy Spirit to help you. He is your Helper, you know! Then, separate your emotions from the situation and try to look at it objectively, asking yourself what is good about the situation and what good can come out of it. Ask yourself what positive qualities and strengths you can develop in response to your set of circumstances. Focus on those things, rather than on how you feel. Finally, stop complaining. I will write to you in Act 2 of this chapter in greater detail about the correlation between your words and your attitude.

For now, I urge you to stop grumbling! One of my favorite songs, written by Reverend Paul Jones says, "all of my good days outweigh my bad days, I won't complain."

We are changed as we change our minds.

You're On

1. What would you consider to be the most important attitude adjustment you need to make right now?

_____

_____

_____

_____

_____

_____

_____

_____

2. In what other areas of your life have you had a bad attitude?

_____

_____

_____

_____

_____

_____

_____

_____

Let me assure you, a new attitude is worth the work!

3. How will you specifically change your attitude in each of the areas you listed in your answer to question 2?

_____

_____

_____

_____

_____

_____

_____

_____

Learn Your Lines

Keep your heart with all diligence,
for out of it spring the issues of life.
Proverbs 4:23

He who disdains instruction despises his own soul,
but he who heeds rebuke gets understanding.
Proverbs 15:32

All the days of the afflicted are evil,
but he who is of a merry heart has a continual feast.
Proverbs 15:15

He who is slothful in his work is a brother
to him who is a great destroyer.
Proverbs 18:9

Let all that you do be done with love.
1 Corinthians 16:14

And let us not grow weary while doing good,
for in due season we shall reap if we do not lose heart.
Galatians 6:9

Rejoice in the Lord always. Again I will say, rejoice!
Philippians 4:4

. . . Comfort the fainthearted, uphold the weak, be patient with all. See that no one renders evil for evil to anyone, but always pursue what is good both for yourselves and for all. Rejoice always, pray without ceasing, in everything give thanks; for this is the will of God in Christ Jesus for you.

1 Thessalonians 5:14b-18

Therefore we also, since we are surrounded by so great a cloud of witnesses, let us lay aside every weight and the sin which so easily ensnares us, and let us run with endurance the race that is set before us.

Hebrews 12:1

Act 2: Out of the Heart the Mouth Speaketh!

One of the best ways to evaluate your attitude is to listen to the words of your mouth. The old King James Version of the Bible says that, "out of the heart the mouth speaketh" (Matt. 12:34), which means that what you say reveals what you think and how you feel. Think about it. When you say, "You know, Sister So-and-So, she just has the best attitude!" how do you know that? You may know this because of the twinkle in her eye or the smile on her face, but you know primarily because of the words she speaks. Similarly, when a person constantly gripes or complains or speaks negatively about people or situations, you may be inclined to say that she has a bad attitude.

> One of the best ways to evaluate your attitude is to listen to the words of your mouth.

Words are powerful. Proverbs 18:21 says "Death and life are in the power of the tongue." Did you know that? The force of your words can either inject death and destruction into a situation or infuse life and hope and courage. When your attitude is positive and full of life, then words of life and blessing will flow out of you. When your attitude is negative and pessimistic, then your talk will be depressing and discouraging.

For that reason, it is imperative to think before you speak. Use your mind before you use your mouth, and don't just pop off and verbalize every thought that enters your brain. Instead, learn to train your tongue by asking yourself some of the following questions before you speak:

◆ Are these words helpful?

◆ Are these words uplifting and encouraging?

◆ Are these words life-giving?

◆ Do these words build up and impart grace?

◆ Do these words indicate a genuine care and concern for the person to whom or about whom I am speaking?

◆ Do these words bring peace and/or joy to a situation?

◆ Would I say these words if Jesus Christ were standing beside me in the flesh?

Death and life are in the power of the tongue, and those who love it will eat its fruit.
Proverbs 18:21

You're On

1. What do your words say about your attitude?

_____

_____

_____

_____

_____

_____

_____

2. What words or phrases do you need to stop saying in order to reflect your new attitude as a leading lady?

_____

_____

_____

_____

_____

_____

_____

3. What positive expressions or biblical confessions can you incorporate into your conversation to encourage yourself and share your positive attitude with others? How can you begin to speak words of life and blessing?

_____

_____

_____

_____

_____

_____

_____

Learn Your Lines

*A wholesome tongue is a tree of life,
but perverseness in it breaks the spirit.*
Proverbs 15:4

*Pleasant words are like a honeycomb,
sweetness to the soul and health to the bones.*
Proverbs 16:24

*The heart of the righteous studies how to answer,
but the mouth of the wicked pours forth evil.*
Proverbs 15:28

*Death and life are in the power of the tongue, and those who
love it will eat its fruit.*
Proverbs 18:21

*Whoever guards his mouth and tongue keeps his soul from
troubles.*
Proverbs 21:23

*Let your speech always be with grace, seasoned with salt, that
you may know how you ought to answer each one.*
Colossians 4:6

COMING SOON

A new attitude will change your entire outlook on life! What changes are you looking forward to? How do you expect the shift in your attitude(s) to positively impact your life?

_____

_____

_____

_____

_____

_____

_____

_____

_____

_____

_____

_____

_____

_____

ACTION!

$\mathcal{B}$ased on what you have learned in this chapter, what are three concise, measurable, attainable goals you will set for yourself in the area of your attitude(s) and the words that reflect your attitude? Be sure to include a schedule and target date for reaching each goal and a reward for accomplishing it.

1. Goal: _____

Schedule and target completion date: _____

Reward: _____

_____

2. Goal: _____

Schedule and target completion date: _____

Reward: _____

_____

3. Goal: _____

Schedule and target completion date: _____

Reward: _____

_____

8

The Lady Chooses Wisely

Introducing

A s a leading lady, you have many decisions to make. Some may be more important than others; some may have significant impact on your own life; some may carry the added weight of affecting other people. When it comes to making good decisions and simply knowing how to live well, there is no substitute for wisdom.

Sometimes we think of wisdom as an ethereal quality that is available only to religious hermits. That couldn't be farther from the truth! Wisdom has been defined as "godly common sense;" it brings peace and joy; and it is available to you right now. In this chapter, I want to help you learn to make wise choices, seek wise counsel, and get wise advice so that your life can be filled with the peace and joy and good judgment that accompany wisdom.

The Main Event

Act 1: The Beginning of Wisdom

Leading ladies are smart enough to know when they have not made wise choices, and if you have lived in this world very long, chances are that you can remember more than one unwise moment in your life! We do learn from our mistakes, but wouldn't it be better not to make the mistakes in the first place? That's why we need wisdom. "But how do I get wisdom?" you may say. I'm glad you asked.

Psalm 111:10 says, "The fear of the Lord is the beginning of wisdom; a good understanding have all those who do His commandments." And James 1:5 says, "If any of you lacks wisdom, let him ask of God, who gives to all liberally and without reproach, and it will be given to him." So you can see that wisdom starts with God; it is primarily a spiritual pursuit, though it can also benefit you mentally and physically.

We do learn from our mistakes, but wouldn't it be better not to make the mistakes in the first place?

Wisdom begins with fearing the Lord and asking Him to give you wisdom. Now, when I use the word *fear*, as in "fear the Lord," I mean to honor Him and to stand in reverential awe of Him. I mean that you admit to Him your utter inability to make wise decisions on your own and your desperate need for the counsel of the Holy Spirit. Not until you approach Him in that kind of humility will true wisdom begin to flow. When you honor Him that way and humbly ask for wisdom, He will give it to you generously!

You're On

1. Do you fear God? I'm serious — do you really stand in awe of Him, or is He just the One to whom you sing on Sunday mornings? Do you have the kind of intimate relationship with Him that allows and invites the wisdom of heaven to flow freely?

_____

_____

_____

_____

_____

_____

> *If any of you lacks wisdom, let him ask of God, who gives to all liberally and without reproach, and it will be given to him.*
>
> **James 1:5**

2. Looking back over your life, what would you consider to be the wisest choice you have ever made?

_____

_____

_____

_____

_____

_____

_____

3. In what areas of your life do you need wisdom right now? How will you begin to seek it?

_____

_____

_____

_____

Learn Your Lines

The law of the Lord is perfect, converting the soul; the testimony of the Lord is sure, making wise the simple.

Psalm 19:7

The fear of the Lord is the beginning of wisdom, and the knowledge of the Holy One is understanding.

Proverbs 9:10

He who trusts his own heart is a fool, but whoever walks wisely will be delivered.

Proverbs 28:26

But you must continue in the things which you have learned and been assured of, knowing from whom you have learned them, and that from childhood you have known the Holy Scriptures, which are able to make you wise for salvation through faith which is in Christ Jesus.

2 Timothy 3:14, 15

Act 2: Walking Wisely Every Day

The Bible says in Proverbs 1:20 that, "Wisdom calls aloud outside; she raises her voice in the open squares." Do you know what that means? It means that wisdom is all around us if we will simply watch for it, and that wisdom can be applied in a variety of practical ways. I need to tell you that there is often wisdom in waiting and in overriding your emotions. I'll give you some examples.

Let's say that you are saving your money to buy a house and you find a house you think you cannot live without. Perhaps you have reached your goal of saving the down payment, but you would be pushed to come up with the money for some of the other expenses involved with buying a house. Do you put all of your money into the house simply because you have the down payment and you love it so much? Your emotions would probably tell you to go ahead and get it before someone else does. Wisdom would ask the following questions (and more!): I have the down payment, but do I have the money for the other costs associated with buying a home? Can I afford the maintenance, the taxes, and the insurance? Can I afford to make the changes I will want to make in order for the house to fit my tastes and lifestyle? Will I be so stretched financially that I cannot meet my other needs or bounce back from an emergency?

Let's use an example from the area of health and nutrition. It is 4:00 in the afternoon and you have a serious case of "the sleepies." You also have a sweet tooth and a weakness for chocolate. You could go to the vending machine and

> *"Wisdom calls aloud outside; she raises her voice in the open squares."*
>
> **Proverbs 1:20**

get a chocolate bar or you could eat an apple. You know the candy bar will give you a quick "sugar rush," but you will then crash! On the other hand, you know the apple will help you feel better gradually, but its affect will last longer and not cause you to sink again. Wisdom chooses the apple!

I think you can begin to see what I mean when I write to you about practical wisdom, so I'll list just a few of the many areas in which you can begin to make wise choices in your everyday life:

> *Wisdom has been defined as "godly common sense;" it brings peace and joy; and it is available to you right now.*

◆ Finances

◆ Social situations

◆ Friendships

◆ Time management

◆ Media and technology influence (how you allow the television you watch, the websites you view, the music you listen to, or the books you read to influence you)

◆ Dating and marriage

◆ Health (exercise, nutrition, and medical care)

◆ Dealing with children

◆ Conversation

◆ Work situations

◆ Conflict resolution

Finally, I want to encourage you to surround yourself with wisdom by seeking wise counsel and good advice. The

Holy Spirit is your first and ultimate source of wisdom, but He often dispenses wisdom through other people. You cannot be your own counselor and advisor all the time — and there is wisdom all around you. When you seek the advice of others, first make sure that the people you are consulting are godly and then make sure that they have a proven track record of success in the area in which you are looking for help. As you seek wisdom in the privacy of your prayer life and in the Word and by soliciting the wise counsel of others, you'll find yourself making better decisions and getting established in God's good plans for you.

You're On

1. In what practical aspect of your life do you most need wisdom right now?

_____

_____

_____

_____

_____

_____

_____

_____

2. In what three areas of the bulleted points listed above can you begin to apply wisdom?

_____

_____

_____

_____

_____

3. What situation in your life could benefit from wise counsel right now? To whom will you turn as you seek wise advice?

_____

_____

_____

_____

_____

_____

_____

Learn Your Lines

Behold, You desire truth in the inward parts,
and in the hidden part You will make me to know wisdom.
Psalm 51:6

So teach us to number our days,
that we may gain a heart of wisdom.
Psalm 90:12

The wise woman builds her house,
but the foolish pulls it down with her hands.
Proverbs 14:1

A fool vents all his feelings,
but a wise man holds them back.
Proverbs 29:11

If the ax is dull, and one does not sharpen the edge,
then he must use more strength;
but wisdom brings success.
Ecclesiastes 10:10

See then that you walk circumspectly,
not as fools but as wise.
Ephesians 5:15

COMING SOON

*C*an you envision living your life and making your decisions according to wisdom? Take a few moments now to think and write about how your life could be different if you were to continually make wise choices.

_____

_____

_____

_____

_____

_____

_____

_____

_____

_____

_____

_____

_____

ACTION!

$\mathcal{B}$ased on what you have learned in this chapter, what are three concise, measurable, attainable goals you will set for yourself when it comes to making wise choices? Be sure to include a schedule and target date for reaching each goal and a reward for accomplishing it.

1. Goal: _____

Schedule and target completion date: _____

Reward: _____

_____

2. Goal: _____

Schedule and target completion date: _____

Reward: _____

_____

3. Goal: _____

Schedule and target completion date: _____

Reward: _____

_____

9

The Lady Knows Her Limits

Introducing

I remember being so excited several years ago when I served as the first female officer of the historic Hampton University Ministers' Conference, which is the largest gathering of African American clergy in the world. As you can imagine, I was extremely busy when it came time for our weeklong annual meeting. My responsibilities were tremendous, and the days were long. I didn't sleep much, and I worked hard, pushing my physical capacity to the limit and allowing no "down time."

Early in the week, I began to feel nauseated, but was too busy to pay much attention to that symptom. The next day, it hit me again, and I had to admit that I could be pregnant. The drug-store test revealed that I was, but I was too busy during that week of meetings to stop and rest or to take care of myself. On the third day of the conference, I began spotting, but I couldn't do anything about it — not until the meetings were finished. By Friday, the spotting increased, but still, I kept going. I returned home that weekend to preach three services, and by Sunday night, you guessed it: no more baby.

I had a miscarriage. I can't tell you all the reasons I lost the baby, but I do know that I pushed myself too hard physically during our ministers' conference. I did not heed the warning signs my body sent me. I went beyond my limits.

I don't want that to happen to you in any area of your life, so let's focus in this chapter on knowing our limits and how to put some boundaries around ourselves so that we are able to bring to life everything God has for us.

The Main Event

Act 1: A Very Personal Question

Miscarriages cannot only happen physically, they can also happen in your life as a whole. It is possible to miscarry your dreams or your destiny, to miscarry a relationship, or to miscarry an opportunity. The end result of any miscarriage is that you do not carry to full-term what has been placed inside of you.

One early warning sign of an impending miscarriage in life is being out of balance. You know what I mean — professional demands take too much time and energy, or you are over-committed at the church, or you spend too many hours watching soap operas, or you are obsessed with getting your body in a shape it isn't meant to be in. Often, being out of balance results from simply being too busy and then thinking you do not have time to take care of yourself, tend your dreams, or nurture your destiny. Let me tell you a story about being out of balance.

While driving in my car one day, I ran over a nail — which, of course, meant my tire would go flat. I pulled into a little tire shop, and the man replaced my old tire with a new one. The car wobbled as I drove, even though the nail had been removed. So, I had to take the car to another shop for an alignment. An alignment puts all the wheels and tires together in synchronization.

Just as my wheels needed to be aligned, we also need an alignment in our lives. We need to be balanced mentally, spiritually, and physically. Prior to the miscarriage I had, I had fallen out of balance. Life was just so busy! I was a pastor; I had a family; I had social obligations; it seemed like every time I turned around, somebody needed something. In the midst of the high-pressure life, I looked good! We had financial stability and all the outer trappings that say "success" to the natural eye. But with all of those things pressing on me and with the push to move faster and faster and do more and more, I began to move myself lower and lower on the priority list. Everything else seemed so urgent that I kept telling myself to wait. I took that attitude at the ministers' conference, and ended up having a miscarriage.

The result of any miscarriage is that you do not carry to full-term what has been placed inside of you.

I want to ask you a very personal question. What has been miscarried in your life? What has God put in you that has not come to birth? What aspects of your destiny have been aborted? What has been lost because you did not take care of yourself in some way? What have you been too busy to nurture? What are the dreams you quit pursuing when more urgent matters arose? (You'll have a chance to write down your answers in the space provided with the questions below.)

One of the joys of our Christian faith is that our God is a *redeeming* God. He is able to turn what the devil meant for bad into something good. He is able to make dead bones spring to life again. He's not only a *redeeming* God, but also a *resurrecting* God and a *restoring* God. He is able to restore the years that have been eaten away. He is able to take your sense of loss and transform it into something that brings deep satisfaction. He just has a way of making things right. He can help you envision your dreams and destiny again and enable you to bring these dreams to life.

You're On

1. Would you answer the very personal question for yourself, right here, in writing? In what areas of your life have you miscarried? Give them to the Lord and ask Him to do a work of restoration in your life.

2. What hopes, plans, or dreams are in jeopardy of being miscarried right now? Why are they being threatened (for instance, you are too busy, you've lost your passion, or you don't believe in yourself anymore)?

_____

_____

_____

_____

_____

_____

_____

One of the joys of our Christian faith is that our God is a redeeming God. He can help you envision your dreams and destiny again and enable you to bring these dreams to life.

3. How can you keep from miscarrying your dreams or your destiny in the future?

_____

_____

_____

_____

_____

_____

_____

_____

_____

Learn Your Lines

But as for you, you meant evil against me;
but God meant it for good, in order to bring it about
as it is this day, to save many people alive.
Genesis 50:20

And He said to me, "Son of man, can these bones live?"
So I answered, "O Lord God, You know." Again He said to me,
"Prophesy to these bones, and say to them, 'O dry bones, hear
the word of the Lord! Thus says the Lord God to these bones:
"Surely I will cause breath to enter into you, and you shall
live. I will put sinews on you and bring flesh upon you, cover
you with skin and put breath in you; and you shall live.
Then you shall know that I am the Lord." ' "
Ezekiel 37:4-6

So I will restore to you the years that the swarming locust has
eaten, the crawling locust, the consuming locust, and the
chewing locust, My great army which I sent among you. You
shall eat in plenty and be satisfied, and praise the name of the
Lord your God, who has dealt wondrously with you; and My
people shall never be put to shame.
Joel 2:25, 26

Act 2: Stay in Your Lane!

The best way I know to keep from getting out of balance is to set boundaries. Now, we all know how beneficial boundaries are on highways. Lanes keep us from getting in the way of other people, and speed limits are intended to keep us from moving too fast. Fender-benders and full-scale collisions occur when the boundaries are not honored. Even then, a seatbelt can minimize the injuries we might sustain — and can even save our lives.

Lanes, speed limits, and seatbelts are all types of boundaries, and they are enforceable by law. Wouldn't it be nice if your personal boundaries were a state law and the police could stop anyone who violated them? Well, that's not the case. Without personal boundaries, you will find yourself forever being crowded out of your own lane by people and circumstances that have no right to push you around. Come on, you know what I mean — that boyfriend who thinks you ought to pay his bills, that boss who continually asks you to do things that are not in your job description, that club or social organization that attempts to lay a guilt trip on you because you do not have time to promote its agenda, that needy friend who pouts when you will not listen to the same ol' sob story for the forty-seventh time. Maybe you do not exercise because you are too busy running children to soccer games. Maybe you do not eat the fruits and vegetables you ought to eat because your family only likes fried food. It is time for a change!

> *Without personal boundaries, you will find yourself forever being crowded out of your own lane by people and circumstances that have no right to push you around.*

You and only you can set and protect your boundaries. You determine how far you will go in relationships, how much time you will spend at the office, how many church activities you will be involved in, how much you will rest, what you will eat, and how you will take care of your body. Only you know the areas of your life where you are stretched too thin or where you are being manipulated, controlled, or influenced to participate in something that isn't good for you or where you are taken advantage of in some way. Only you know if you are suffering from what I call "spiritual osteoporosis," which is when you are so bent over from carrying everybody else's load and helping so many people with their problems that you can hardly walk.

My sister, it may be time for you to tell everybody else to carry their own stuff. It may be time for you to sit on a bench somewhere and turn down those countless opportunities to help people so that you can begin to focus on getting your life back into balance. It may be time for you to leave the situations that are not healthy for you — a relationship, a work environment, any place where you are being abused in any way. It may be time to tell the family that you are making steamed broccoli for supper and that those who don't like it can fix their own dinner!

Then again, maybe you are doing okay — not necessarily needing to slam on the brakes, but perhaps needing to slow down. Your life may need a caution light more than it needs a stoplight. You may need to delegate some of your

> *You and only you can set and protect your boundaries. You determine how far you will go in relationships, how much time you will spend at the office, how many church activities you will be involved in, how much you will rest, what you will eat, and how you will take care of your body.*

responsibilities because you can tell that your load is getting too heavy. You have to pace your life according to the "speed limit" the Lord has given you. It may also be time for you to simply slow down, because when you are moving too fast, you are much more likely to overstep your boundaries, to drive outside your lanes — and that is your safety zone.

Whatever your situation, God knows what your boundaries need to be. I encourage you to seek Him and ask Him what you are to do. You'll find wisdom in His Word, and you won't fail when your life is aligned with the Scriptures. He has given you your limits; He knows how much you can handle. David realized this when he wrote in Psalm 16:6, "The lines have fallen to me in pleasant places . . ." So ask; He'll let you know how far you can go in every situation.

Once your boundaries are in place, you will be in infinitely better shape to carry on your life and to fulfill your destiny. In fact, that's really the only way you can. A leading lady knows when she is in her divinely appointed place, but she also knows when she is out of place. The only way to hear the cues of life and to perform with star quality is to determine the boundaries that are right for you and then to live within them. Be your own boundary police!

You're On

1. In what areas of your life do you not have good boundaries?

_____

_____

_____

_____

_____

_____

2. Where do you need to completely stop and put down your load so that you can re-evaluate everything you are doing? In what areas do you simply need to slow down so that you will not crash?

_____

_____

_____

_____

_____

_____

3. What steps are you going to take in order to develop healthy boundaries in each of the areas you have listed in the questions above?

_____

_____

_____

_____

_____

_____

Learn Your Lines

So Moses' father-in-law said to him, "The thing that you do is not good. Both you and these people who are with you will surely wear yourselves out. For this thing is too much for you; you are not able to perform it by yourself."

Exodus 18:17, 18

*To everything there is a season,
a time for every purpose under heaven.*

Ecclesiastes 3:1

*But those who wait on the Lord shall renew their strength;
they shall mount up with wings like eagles, they shall run
and not be weary; they shall walk and not faint.*

Isaiah 40:31

COMING SOON

*S*etting boundaries will change your life for the better. It's like building a fence around yourself to keep out those things that could harm you and to keep you from going outside the limits the Lord has given you. What are you looking forward to as you begin to learn not to overextend yourself? For instance, are you anticipating strengthened relationships or the sense of empowerment that comes from saying, "No"? Do you smile when you think about how happy and free you are going to be when you no longer feel manipulated on the job or stretched too thin by social obligations? What dreams need to be dusted off in your mind? What aspects of your destiny will you attend to again once your life regains its balance?

ACTION!

*B*ased on what you have learned in this chapter, what are three concise, measurable, attainable goals you will set for yourself in the area of boundaries? Be sure to include a schedule and target date for reaching each goal and a reward for accomplishing it.

1. Goal: _____

Schedule and target completion date: _____

Reward: _____

_____

2. Goal: _____

Schedule and target completion date: _____

Reward: _____

_____

3. Goal: _____

Schedule and target completion date: _____

Reward: _____

_____

10

The Lady Stops

Introducing

had been pastoring for seven years when the phone call came. In the seventh year of my pastorate, God gave me a gift. I received a phone call from Harvard University Divinity School. The administration there told me about a wonderful program they were offering, and asked me to join their team of administrators. *What a great opportunity*, I thought! But it was not only a great opportunity; it was a gift from God. You see, I was burned out. I was stressed out and worn out and in desperate need of a change of pace. I felt like Humpty Dumpty — so broken that I could not be put back together again.

The opportunity at Harvard would require me to leave the pastorate for one year, to move away from the hustle and bustle of New York's inner city, and to spend twelve glorious months on Harvard's beautiful campus in Cambridge, Massachusetts. The Lord gave me a sabbatical, during which He did begin to put me back together again. He spoke to me, poured into me, brought new people into my life, and birthed this ministry of wholeness and balance that I now enjoy. He allowed me to stop everything I had been doing for the previous seven years and find rest and renewal.

Prior to that point, I had not done a good job of integrating times of refreshment into my busy life. Maybe that's why He gave me an entire year! But because He gave me that gift and taught me the lessons of taking a break, I want to share some of them with you.

The Main Event

Act 1: Don't Be a Pothole Sister

I once drove a blue Volvo with cream-colored leather seats. That car was more than just a means of transportation for me; it was also a satellite office, a nail salon, a worship center, a dressing room, a breakfast nook, and a make-up station! Like you, I have a busy life and I move quickly — sometimes I go the speed limit and sometimes I don't (not that I'm proud of that. I'm just honest with you!). One day, when I was driving down the highway at a higher-than-usual speed; I saw a pothole several yards ahead of me. Even though I saw it, I could not avoid it. Oh, I hit it hard. The whole car shook as my wheel fell into that hole, but I somehow managed to get out and keep moving. If I had slowed down, I could have missed the pothole, but I was a woman on the go, you know, and I didn't have time to go slowly.

Fast-forward about three weeks. I was driving down the highway again and turned my steering wheel to the left. In full rebellion, my car veered to the right. I turned harder to the left; it veered more to the right. Before too long, my car began to shake like a washing

> *Because I had not taken the car into the shop immediately after my run-in with the pothole, what could have been a $300 repair bill became a $1,700 expense. How expensive are your life lessons?*

machine on the spin cycle. At that point, I made my way to the car dealer and ended up in a conversation that went something like this:

Technician: "You hit a pothole, didn't you?"

Me: "Yes."

Technician: "And you've been driving this car for weeks, haven't you?"

Me: "Ummm, yes."

The technician then proceeded to inform me that because I had not taken the car into the shop immediately after my run-in with the pothole that what could have been a $300 repair bill became a $1,700 expense. Because I had continued to drive a slightly damaged car, one problem had led to another, and my car now needed a significant amount of work.

> *Dealing daily with the stresses of life is one of the best pieces of advice I can give you — and it's necessary if you are going to live a healthy, balanced life.*

Sound familiar? Have you ever let something go so long that it ended up being a much bigger challenge than it should have been? Have you ever neglected a problem to the point that it started producing more problems and ended up in a complicated mess? Then you might be a Pothole Sister.

What is a Pothole Sister? Simply this: a woman who does not take care of herself and does not tend to situations as they arise. Potholes happen in our lives the same way they happen on the highway. They tend to show up after a snowstorm or after icy conditions, in places where the road has eroded and has undergone too much wear and tear. In those places, the road cannot handle the pressure of the snow and ice, so it just caves in. Similarly, there are places in our lives that are stressed — and when the storms of life come, they are not strong enough to resist the pressure. Then we cave in.

I wonder, my sister: has that ever happened to you? Taking care of roads every day in order to avoid potholes would be impossible for construction crews to do, but taking care of yourself daily is possible. In fact, dealing daily with the stresses of life is one of the best pieces of advice I can give you — and it's necessary if you are going to live a healthy, balanced life.

You're On

1. Where are the potholes or potential potholes in your life?

_____

_____

_____

_____

_____

Even our Father took a break and rested from His work. And if He needed a Sabbath, I can guarantee that you do, too!

_____

_____

_____

_____

_____

_____

2. How did you hit those potholes — what pressures have been building up, what conflicts are unresolved, what matters have gone unattended?

_____

_____

_____

_____

_____

_____

_____

3. Why haven't you had your personal pothole(s) fixed yet?

_____

_____

_____

_____

_____

_____

I urge you to set aside one day a week in which you will rest from your labors, have some fun, enjoy yourself, seek God, and allow the Holy Spirit to refresh you.

Learn Your Lines

*Evening and morning and at noon I will pray
and cry aloud, and He shall hear my voice.*

Psalm 55:17

*So I will sing praise to Your name forever,
that I may daily perform my vows.*

Psalm 61:8

Do not let the sun go down on your wrath . . .

Ephesians 4:26

Act 2: Your Personal Stop Day

If you are a Pothole Sister, I have good news for you! God's design for our lives includes a built-in day of rest, during which you can re-fuel and re-charge and gain new strength for the busy week ahead. As you learn to deal with the trials and challenges of your life, I believe you will notice an increase in inner peace and find your stress level decreasing. In addition, a regular "Stop Day" (what the Bible calls "the Sabbath") will give you opportunity to simply rest — and hopefully remove yourself from some of the pressure-packed situations that arise during the work week or during your busy days at home.

Even our Father took a break and rested from His work. And if He needed a Sabbath, I can guarantee that you do, too! God says in many places in His Word that you can be repaired, restored, revived, and renewed. He leads you beside the still waters, so that He can restore your soul (Ps. 23:2, 3).

Just as a mechanic cannot repair a car that is racing down the highway, it is difficult to be restored and renewed if you are not at rest. Now I realize that your lifestyle or profession may prohibit your using Sunday as your Sabbath Day, but I urge you to set aside one day a week in which you will rest from your labors, have some fun, enjoy yourself, seek God, and allow the Holy Spirit to refresh you.

You're On

1. Be honest with me. Do you regularly observe the Sabbath and take seriously your need for rest and rejuvenation?

_____

_____

_____

_____

_____

_____

_____

2. If you answered "yes," to question 1, I'm proud of you! You can skip the other 2 questions. If you answered "no," above, why are you not taking care of yourself in this way?

_____

_____

_____

_____

_____

_____

3. What changes are you going to make in your life in order to incorporate a personal Stop Day?

_____

_____

_____

_____

_____

_____

_____

_____

Learn Your Lines

Remember the Sabbath day, to keep it holy.
Exodus 20:8

Keep sound wisdom and discretion; so they will be life
to your soul and grace to your neck. Then you will walk
safely in your way, and your foot will not stumble.
When you lie down you will not be afraid; yes,
you will lie down and your sleep will be sweet.
Proverbs 3:21b-24

And He said to them, "The Sabbath was made for man,
and not man for the Sabbath."
Mark 2:27

Therefore, since a promise remains of entering His rest,
let us fear lest any of you seem to have come short of it.
Hebrews 4:1

Be still, and know that I am God.
Psalm 46:10

COMING SOON

Once you learn to deal with the stresses of your life on a daily basis, your life will be different — healthier, more relaxed, more balanced. As you look toward beginning to live that way, what are you looking forward to? And, what will you do with the renewed energy and strength that will come as you develop a new routine that includes a regular Sabbath?

ACTION!

*B*ased on what you have learned in this chapter, what are three concise, measurable, attainable goals you will set for yourself as you think about avoiding life's potholes and about the rest and rejuvenation you need? Be sure to include a schedule and target date for reaching each goal and a reward for accomplishing it.

1. Goal: _____

Schedule and target completion date: _____

Reward: _____

_____

2. Goal: _____

Schedule and target completion date: _____

Reward: _____

_____

3. Goal: _____

Schedule and target completion date: _____

Reward: _____

_____

The Lady in the Know

The following chapters address specific health issues that are especially important to women. I really want you to be informed about these diseases and conditions, so that you can know your risk factors and identify the warning signs. Hopefully, a little education will help you guard against these things and stay healthy.

I'll change our format slightly in these chapters. For instance, we will not include a "Coming Soon" section. (I had a hard time envisioning you writing down your dreams about colon health!) Also, instead of Bible verses to memorize in the "Learn Your Lines" section, I have listed some "Supporting Roles" at the end of each chapter so that you will know where to find further information on these issues.

11

The Lady and Her Heart

Introducing

The Bible has a lot to say about our hearts. Granted, most of the time it is referring to a condition of the heart — an attitude or belief — and not to the heart as a physical organ, but there's no doubt our attitudes, beliefs, and conditions of the heart do affect our physical health. For instance, take a look at these Bible verses that make the connection between a happy, whole heart and physical health:

- A sound heart is life to the body, but envy is rottenness to the bones (Prov. 14:30).

- A merry heart makes a cheerful countenance, but by sorrow of heart the spirit is broken (Prov. 15:13).

- A merry heart does good like medicine, but a broken spirit dries the bones (Prov. 17:22).

My hope for you is that, through this workbook, your heart has been healed and made whole and that the promises of the Word listed above are being manifested in your life.

Nevertheless, heart disease threatens women, and I want you to be informed about it.

The Main Event

Act 1: Facing the Facts

Not only is heart disease a silent killer; it's also America's most deadly disease. One out of every 2.5 deaths (39%) in the United States can be attributed to two types of cardio-vascular disease: heart disease and stroke. They, along with other forms of cardiovascular disease, such as high blood pressure and angina (chest pain), kill a staggering 945,000 Americans each year — 2,600 a day, which amounts to a rate of one death every 33 seconds. Every year, cardio-vascular disease kills more than 500,000 women. Needless to say, the statistics are sobering.

> *Every year in the United States, more than 500,000 women die of cardiovascular disease (source: Time, 4/28/03, p. 61).*

Yet mention the words *heart disease* or *stroke*, and most people think of an older, overweight man gripping his chest in sudden pain. The truth is, heart disease is the leading cause of death among women in America and accounts for half of all deaths of women over age 50. And no one is at greater risk than African American women. In 2000, the National Center for Health Statistics reported that cardiovascular disease made up almost 41% of all deaths among African American women.

The term *heart disease* is used to describe several disorders involving the heart and circulatory system. Heart attack, angina, irregular heartbeat, and coronary artery disease

(CAD) are all ailments of this disease. While women have much less chance of experiencing heart disease before age 50 than men, menopause changes these odds significantly. By age 65, one in four women struggles with some form of heart disease. Clearly, this is no longer just a man's disease.

You're On

1. What is America's most deadly killer? What is the leading cause of death among women in America?

_____

_____

_____

_____

_____

_____

2. How many women die of cardiovascular disease each year?

_____

_____

_____

_____

"The more scientists learn about a woman's heart and what can go wrong with it, the more they realize that females aren't just small males. There are subtle but important differences in how women's cardiovascular systems respond to stress, hormones, excess saturated fat and toxins like tobacco." (Time, 4/28/03, p. 62)

3. By age 65, how many women struggle with some form of heart disease?

_____

_____

_____

_____

_____

_____

_____

_____

Act 2: Addressing the Problem

Like an enemy scouting out its target, heart disease clearly and definitely profiles its victims. If you are overweight, physically inactive, or smoke, or if you have high blood pressure, high blood cholesterol levels, or diabetes, consider yourself a target of this deadly disease.

Those who are overweight put themselves at immediate risk because of the linking factors. The more you weigh, the harder you make your heart work, which causes your blood pressure to rise. This can affect your blood cholesterol levels, which in turn can possibly lead to diabetes. Along with this, if you remain overweight or physically inactive, your heart loses its ability to drive the circulatory system, straining more to pump the same amount of blood throughout the body.

While smoking has always been linked with lung cancer, the fact is that one and a half times as many tobacco smokers die from heart disease, rather than lung disease. If you smoke, your chances of a heart attack increases two to six times more than a non-smoker. Put simply, smoking automatically makes you a prime candidate for heart disease — along with many other diseases.

Although these are all controllable risk factors, there are some inherent, uncontrollable variables for developing heart disease: race, age, and heredity. Unfortunately, African Americans have almost twice as much chance of developing heart disease than any other race, primarily because of a genetic tendency toward more extreme hypertension (high blood pressure). Age also plays a major factor; older women (post-menopause) have almost twice as great a chance of experiencing some form of heart disease. In addition, those whose parents battled heart disease are more susceptible to developing it themselves.

Despite the many risk factors and the grim statistics proving the seriousness of heart disease, you can decrease your chances of developing it if you make simple, healthy lifestyle changes. Unlike many other diseases, most of the major risk factors for heart disease can be controlled. Smoking is a

"Heart disease is the No. 1 killer of women, yet only 8% of American women realize it is a greater threat than cancer. A woman has a 50% chance of dying from her first heart attack, compared with a 30% chance for a man. Of those who survive their first heart attack, 38% of women will die within a year vs. 25% of men. 46% of women are disabled by heart failure after heart attack, compared with 22% of men." (Time, 4/28/03, pp. 64-65)

choice; the longer you continue, the more at risk of heart disease you become each day. And while changing to low-tar and low-nicotine cigarettes may reduce your chance of developing other diseases such as lung cancer, it does nothing to affect the risk of heart disease.

By the same token, being overweight or obese drastically increases your chances of developing this deadly disease, for all the aforementioned reasons. If you are currently overweight and aren't on a weight-loss plan or an exercise program, consult your doctor about beginning both. For the average person, losing 10 to 20 pounds can significantly reduce her chances of developing heart disease, so start by setting small goals to lose weight. Exercise daily and watch your eating habits, paying special attention to your fat intake. (Choose unsaturated fats over saturated fats.)

> *For the average person, losing 10 to 20 pounds can significantly reduce her chances of developing heart disease, so start by setting small goals to lose weight.*

These changes will in turn affect your blood pressure, which needs to be checked regularly if you are overweight. If your blood pressure stays above 140/90 mmHg for a considerable period of time, it's time for a visit to your doctor. It's possible for older women to develop heart disease with blood pressure lower than this, so keep an eye on both numbers. Any major difference between the numbers signals an increased risk. A simple way to lower your blood pressure is to consume less sodium, replacing this with food high in potassium, which is particularly effective in the fight against high blood pressure. Add an additional portion of vegetables or fruit to your diet; this will provide more of the nutrients such as calcium and magnesium that your blood needs. And when cooking, avoid using a lot of salt, flavoring your dishes instead with herbs and non-sodium spices.

Finally, have your cholesterol level checked regularly. Your goal is to maintain a cholesterol level of lower than 200 mg/dL (milligrams per deciliter). Anything over 240 mg/dL warrants a trip to the doctor and some lifestyle changes. However, there are two factors to assessing your risk of heart disease when it comes to cholesterol levels: high-density lipoprotein (HDL) and low-density lipoprotein (LDL). HDL is considered the "good" cholesterol; it aids in creating a clear, flowing passageway of blood to the arteries. LDL, on the other hand, can eventually block these passageways if it builds up. To avoid risk of heart disease, aim for an HDL level of less than 35 mg/dL and an LDL level below 130 mg/dL. Besides advising you to watch your intake of high-cholesterol food, your doctor can instruct you on other ways to maintain desirable levels of each type of cholesterol.

Heart disease may be a deadly disease, but it's also a preventable one. If you are an African American woman, you are a prime target — and the older you get, the more your chances increase for developing heart disease. With simple, healthy lifestyle changes, and the assistance of your doctor, you can avoid becoming a heart disease statistic.

You're On

1. Which risk factors for heart disease can you identify in your life?

_____

_____

_____

_____

_____

_____

2. How long has it been since you have had your cholesterol checked? Will you plan to have that done soon? (Sometimes a local hospital, YMCA, or senior citizens center will offer this service.)

_____

_____

_____

_____

_____

_____

3. What lifestyle changes will you make to minimize your risk?

_____

_____

_____

_____

Supporting Roles

Websites

Heart.org

Heartsupport.com

Heartinfo.org

MayoClinic.com

Blackwomenshealth.org

(This is the website for the Black Women's Health Imperative, founded in 1983 by health activist Byllye Y. Avery. It is the leading African American women's health education, research, advocacy, and leadership development institution)

Books

Before the Heart Attacks
Robert Superko and Laura Tucker
Rodale Press
June 2003

Take a Load Off Your Heart:
114 Things You Can Do to Prevent or Reverse Heart Disease
Barry Franklin
Joseph C. Piscatella
Barry A. Franklin
Workman Publishing Company
February 2003

The Healthy Heart Cookbook
Health Magazine Editors
Oxmoor House
January 2003

The Mayo Clinic Heart Book
Bernard J. Gersh
William Morrow
2nd edition – January 2000

ACTION!

*B*ased on what you have learned in this chapter, what are three concise, measurable, attainable goals you will set for yourself in the area of heart health? Goals may be as simple and practical as having your cholesterol checked and keeping an eye on your blood pressure every week, or setting goals for gradual weight loss and thereby reducing your risk for heart disease. Be sure to include a schedule and target date for reaching each goal and a reward for accomplishing it.

1. Goal: _____

Schedule and target completion date: _____

Reward: _____

_____

2. Goal: _____

Schedule and target completion date: _____

Reward: _____

_____

3. Goal: _____

Schedule and target completion date: _____

Reward: _____

_____

12

The Lady and Colon Health

Introducing

t's not exactly a topic you'd bring up at a dinner party. In fact, most people would rather avoid talking about it altogether. Yet colorectal cancer (cancer of the colon or rectum) is more than just a serious issue in need of being addressed. For many, it's a life or death matter. As the second leading cause of cancer deaths in the United States and third most common cancer around the world, colorectal cancer is a disease that cannot be shied away from.

The common belief is that colorectal cancer is a man's disease. But the truth is that it is no respecter of persons; it cares not if you are a man or woman. Because of the stigma surrounding colorectal cancer, many women avoid being tested for it or even asking their doctor about it. The result can be needless death; colorectal cancer is a completely preventable disease if caught early. If you or someone you know shows any symptoms of colorectal cancer or exhibits any of the risk factors mentioned in this chapter, consult a doctor about being tested. Forget the stigma and save a life — possibly yours.

The Main Event

Act 1: Facing the Facts

In case you haven't taken colorectal cancer seriously enough in the past, here's all you should know: When detected early, colorectal cancer is completely curable. Yet one out of every two people diagnosed with the disease will die. Given the improvements in general cancer treatment within the past two decades, this indicates a tragedy — that almost half of the reported cases resulted in death simply because people were ashamed to be tested soon enough.

This year, almost 57,000 Americans will die from colorectal cancer, while an estimated 147,000 new cases will be diagnosed. Cancer of the colon will cause about 48,100 deaths and rectal cancer about 8,500 deaths. Colorectal cancer is the third most common cancer diagnosed for both sexes (excluding skin cancers). One in four people remain at risk of getting it because of either age or other risk factors.

> *Colorectal cancer is a completely preventable disease if caught early. When detected early, it is completely curable.*

Proven in all these statistics is the fact that this isn't just a man's disease, as it has been known in the past. In fact, more women are found with cancer of the colon than men. More women over the age of 75 die from colorectal cancer than from breast cancer. And as is the case with almost every cancer, African American women rank the highest among all populations in deaths due to colon and rectal cancer. The death rate from colorectal cancer among all African Americans is 30% higher than that for Caucasians.

Most experts agree that the primary reason for this is a lack of screening for the disease.

The good news is that the numbers of new cases and deaths due to colorectal cancer are both declining. In fact, the death rate from this disease has gone down over the past two decades, likely because of earlier screening. When the cancer is caught early and not given the chance to spread, patients have a 90% survival rate for the five years following their diagnosis. If the cancer spreads to nearby organs, the survival rate lowers to 65%. And sadly, if the cancer spreads to distant parts of the body, such as the liver or lungs, the odds plummet to a 9% chance. Clearly, early diagnosis is the key, yet unfortunately only 37% of colorectal cancers are discovered in the initial stages.

More women over the age of 75 die from colorectal cancer than from breast cancer.

Colorectal cancer develops slowly, taking almost 10 years to significantly progress. This obviously provides the opportunity for individuals to find the most common indicator of colorectal cancer, a polyp, early in its growth. Polyps are wart-like growths found along the wall of the large intestine, which serves as part of your digestive system to remove and process nutrients and pass waste out of your body. Within the large intestine are the colon and rectum. As these polyps form, they range from the hyperplastic type (which are less than 5 mm in size) to the adenomas (their size can vary, but often they become more cancerous as they grow). Not every polyp is cancerous — only one in seven is — but almost all colon cancers begin as polyps.

While these often begin without symptoms, there are a few possible signs to indicate colorectal cancer:

◆ blood (bright red or dark) in the stool

◆ change in bowel habits

◆ unexplainable weight loss

◆ frequent exhaustion

◆ diarrhea, constipation, or feeling that the bowel doesn't completely empty

◆ vomiting

◆ narrow stools

◆ frequent abdominal discomfort (gas pains, bloating, fullness, or cramps) from iron deficiency anemia

You're On

1. What is the third most common cancer diagnosed in both men and women?

_____

_____

_____

_____

_____

2. Are you embarrassed to be tested for colorectal disease? If so, would you please get over it and take responsibility for this area of your health?

_____

_____

_____

_____

_____

_____

3. What are three possible warning signs of colorectal cancer? Do you have any of these? If so, call your doctor!

_____

_____

_____

_____

_____

African American women rank the highest among all populations in deaths due to colon and rectal cancer.

4. Does this form of cancer run in your family?

_____

_____

_____

_____

_____

_____

_____

_____

_____

Act 2: Addressing the Problem

As with any cancer, there are known factors that increase your risk for being diagnosed with colorectal cancer:

◆ Age. About 90% of people with colorectal cancer are age 50 or older.

◆ Family history of colorectal cancer.

◆ Family history of adenomatous polyposis or nonpolyposis cancer (such as Lynch Syndrome).

◆ Personal history of cancer of the colon, rectum, ovary, endometrium, or breast.

◆ Personal history of inflammatory bowel disease (such as ulcerative colitis and Crohn's disease).

◆ History of polyps or ulcers in the large intestine.

◆ Smoking.

◆ Diet. Studies indicate that a high-fat, low-fiber diet increases your risk of colorectal cancer.

◆ Physical inactivity. If you live a sedentary lifestyle, you increase your risk for colon cancer.

While there is nothing you can do about your family history of colorectal cancer or about the increased risk that comes with being over 50 years of age, there are certain things you can do to prevent the onset of this disease. Following are some basic lifestyle changes that can lower your risk for cancer of the colon or rectum:

◆ Eat foods from plant sources. Include at least five servings of vegetables and fruits daily.

◆ Avoid foods high in fat.

◆ Ensure you're getting an adequate daily amount of calcium. Take a dietary supplement if needed.

◆ Use alcohol moderately, if at all.

◆ Don't use tobacco products.

◆ Eat foods high in fiber.

◆ Exercise regularly.

◆ Lose weight, if needed.

> *As a woman, you may think your visit to the gynecologist is enough if he or she checks your rectal area. However, it's not; if you're over 50, you still need to have a fecal occult blood test every year.*

As a woman, you may think your visit to the gynecologist is enough if he or she checks your rectal area. However, it's not; if you're over 50, you still need to have a fecal occult blood test every year. This is simply an examination of your stool sample for hidden blood. Studies show that the death rate from colorectal cancer for those who have this test yearly lowers by 30%. In addition to the annual fecal occult blood test, you should follow through with the following tests if you are over 50 years old:

◆ Sigmoidoscopy. This is when a doctor looks inside your lower colon and rectum for any polyps, potential cancer growths, or abnormalities. You should have a sigmoidoscopy when you turn 50 and every five years after that.

◆ Barium enema. Despite the bad rap of an enema, this is an effective way to detect any polyps or abnormalities in the lower colon and rectum. An x-ray of the lower gastrointestinal tract is taken by using a barium-containing liquid inserted into the rectum. You should get a barium enema every five to 10 years.

◆ Colonoscopy. Considered the most effective test for detecting colon cancer, this procedure is similar to a sigmoidoscopy but done by a board-certified gastroenterologist who exams the entire colon and rectum. While a colonoscopy involves some minor risks, it should be taken every 10 years.

In addition, a digital rectal examination should be part of each screening. This is simply when a doctor or nurse feels for any lumps or abnormalities and also collects a stool sample to check for blood. Note: If someone in your family aged

60 years or younger has had colorectal cancer, a more intensive screening may be needed than a sigmoidoscopy. As always, consult your doctor.

You're On

1. Which risk factors for colorectal cancer can you identify in your life?

_____

_____

_____

_____

_____

_____

2. If you are over 50, have you had the necessary examinations described above? If not, when will you see the doctor and take responsibility for your colon health?

_____

_____

_____

_____

_____

_____

9. What lifestyle changes will you make to minimize your risk?

_____

_____

_____

_____

_____

_____

_____

_____

_____

Supporting Roles

Websites

Cancer.org

Cancer.gov

Cancerfacts.com

MayoClinic.com

Books

Tell Me What to Eat to Prevent Colon Cancer
Elaine Magee
New Page Books
February 2001

100 Questions and Answers about Colon Cancer
David A. Bub, Susannah Rose, W. Douglas Wong
Jones and Bartlett Publishers
November 2002

Understanding Colon Cancer
A. Richard Adrouny, M.D., F.A.C.P.
University Press of Mississippi
July 2002

ACTION!

*B*ased on what you have learned in this chapter, what are three concise, measurable, attainable goals you will set for yourself in the area of colon health? Your goals may be as simple as making sure that you schedule your next check-up or that you reduce some of the risks you have learned about in this chapter (for instance, eating at least five servings of vegetables and fruits per day). Be sure to include a schedule and target date for reaching each goal and a reward for accomplishing it.

1. Goal: _____

Schedule and target completion date: _____

Reward: _____

_____

2. Goal: _____

Schedule and target completion date: _____

Reward: _____

_____

3. Goal: _____

Schedule and target completion date: _____

Reward: _____

_____

13

The Lady and Diabetes

Introducing

God has a habit of turning potentially horrific situations into testimonies of grace. He does it with our lives, and He does it with our experiences. For every dark corner we back ourselves into, He awaits the time to recreate the scene into a beaming, living showcase of His power to change, to heal, and to love. His light changes everything.

So it is with diabetes. What seems like a debilitating disease that by the numbers may shackle your quality of life can actually be a lesson in how to overcome trials. As a black woman, you are a prime target for diabetes, especially as you get older. My mother had diabetes, so I'm especially connected to this chapter.

Yet whether you're facing the prospect of being diagnosed with diabetes or are simply trying to take the proper precautions to avoid it, simple lifestyle changes can help illuminate your path to health. With God's guidance toward a healthier lifestyle, you can avoid the darkness.

The Main Event

Act 1: Facing the Facts

Diabetes needs no introduction. Unfortunately, the disturbing numbers surrounding the disease speak for themselves:

♦ Approximately 17 million people in the United States — 6.2% of the population — have diabetes. While 11.1 million have been diagnosed, the remaining 5.9 million people are unaware they have diabetes — an amazing one out of three people.

♦ More than 800,000 new cases of diabetes are diagnosed each year.

♦ Diabetes is the fifth-leading cause of death, with more than 210,000 fatalities each year.

♦ Diabetes is the leading cause of blindness in adults ages 20 to 74.

♦ Diabetes increases the risk of both heart disease and stroke by 200 to 400%.

♦ 60 to 65% of diabetics have high blood pressure.

♦ 40% of people who suffer from kidney failure are diabetic.

Still unfamiliar with the seriousness of diabetes? It's time to educate yourself. Approximately 2.8 million (or 13%) of all African Americans have diabetes — a percentage twice as large as every other race but Hispanics. And the mortality rates among black men and women are 20 and 40% higher, respectively, than their white counterparts. Not only do a larger percentage of African Americans have diabetes, a significantly greater segment also suffers debilitating complications from the disease, such as kidney failure, eye disease, amputations, gum disease, and heart disease.

Approximately 9.1 million (or 8.9%) of all adult women in the United States have diabetes. Yet a staggering one in four black women over the age of 55 has the disease. In virtually every category, black women lead the pack in both susceptibility to diabetes and diabetic complications. From increased risk of heart disease to toxemia to pregnancy complications to peripheral vascular disease, African American women seem to have two strikes against them before ever entering the game. If you are an African American woman, this is something you should take action against.

Diabetes is a disease in which the body does not produce or properly use insulin. Insulin is a hormone needed to convert carbohydrates, sugars, and proteins into blood glucose, which we use for energy. There are four major types of diabetes:

Approximately 9.1 million (or 8.9%) of all adult women in the United States have diabetes. Yet a staggering one in four black women over the age of 55 has the disease. In virtually every category, black women lead the pack in both susceptibility to diabetes and diabetic complications.

◆ Type 1 — develops when the body's immune system destroys pancreatic beta cells, the only cells in the body that make insulin. Type 1 diabetes accounts for only 5 to 10% of all diabetes cases, is more common among children and young adults, and involves required insulin injections for survival.

◆ Type 2 — develops when the body fails to properly use insulin and/or produces an insufficient amount of insulin. The majority of diabetics (90 to 95%) suffer from type 2.

◆ Gestational — is diagnosed during pregnancy when a woman develops glucose intolerance or has elevated blood glucose levels. It requires treatment to stabilize the woman's blood glucose levels in order to protect her baby. Although these levels usually return to normal after pregnancy, a woman has a significantly greater chance of developing Type 2 diabetes over the following 5 to 10 years. Gestational diabetes is 80% more common in African Americans than in Caucasians.

◆ Prediabetes — occurs when a person's blood glucose levels are higher than normal levels but still below type 2 levels. While 17 million Americans have diabetes, an estimated additional 16 million have prediabetes.

Without a thorough examination, diabetes is often difficult to detect because whereas some diabetics show common symptoms, others do not. Despite this, the following symptoms merit consulting your doctor:

◆ extreme thirst

◆ frequent urination

◆ unexplained weight loss

◆ increased appetite

Despite the serious threat of diabetes, this doesn't have to be a debilitating disease. Hundreds of thousands of diabetics lead productive, satisfying lives due to taking care of themselves through means as simple as healthy eating, exercising, and monitoring their blood glucose levels.

- blurred vision
- sores that don't heal

Despite the serious threat of diabetes, this doesn't have to be a debilitating disease. Hundreds of thousands of diabetics lead productive, satisfying lives due to taking care of themselves through means as simple as eating healthily, exercising, and monitoring their blood glucose levels.

You're On

1. Diabetes increases the risk of heart attack or stroke by how much?

_____

_____

_____

2. What is the leading cause of blindness in adults, ages 20-74?

_____

_____

_____

3. What are three symptoms that should be reported to your doctor if you develop them?

_____

_____

_____

Act 2: Addressing the Problem

Regardless of how threatening diabetes can sound, the truth is that it can be held in check by taking precautions and making a few lifestyle changes. One of the first precautions to take is becoming aware of the risk factors that increase the chance of developing diabetes. These are

◆ family history of diabetes

◆ high cholesterol

◆ obesity or overweight condition (especially excess upper-body weight)

◆ prediabetes — when a person already has higher blood glucose levels than normal but lower than type 2 diabetes

◆ high blood pressure

◆ gestational diabetes — another case of semi-diabetic conditions; women who develop gestational diabetes through pregnancy have an increased chance of developing full type 2 diabetes

◆ hyperinsulinemia — condition of higher-than-normal levels of fasting insulin, which can lead to type 2 diabetes

- age — at age 40, the risk of developing diabetes increases significantly

- physical inactivity

If you currently have at least two of these conditions, consult your doctor about a diabetes test, which simply involves measuring the amount of glucose in your blood sample. If you've already been diagnosed with diabetes, the following guidelines can help you manage your condition:

Regardless of how threatening diabetes can sound, the truth is that it can be held in check by taking precautions and making a few lifestyle changes.

- Check your blood sugar levels. This is the most important preventative measure for reducing the chance of complications from diabetes. Your doctor can advise you on how often you should check your levels and how to record them.

- Eat well-balanced meals. Keeping a healthy diet including proper portions of each of the four main food groups (fruits and vegetables/whole grains, cereals and bread/dairy products/meats, fish, poultry, eggs, beans, and nuts) will help you manage your weight.

- Watch your fat and cholesterol intake. Foods high in fat such as whole dairy products, red meat, and most desserts should be either avoided or eaten in moderation. Gaining control of your cholesterol and lipid count can also reduce heart disease by up to 50%.

- Take care of your feet. Ask your doctor about a foot care program to ensure healthy circulation in both feet.

◆ Keep an eye on your eyes. Since blindness is one of the many possible complications of diabetes, schedule regular check-ups with your optometrist.

◆ Avoid foods high in sugar. This is a no-brainer for any diabetic.

◆ Exercise. Directly related to your weight control, keeping your body in good shape can lower your blood glucose level while also enhancing the effects of your body's natural insulin supply. In a recent survey, researchers found that 50% of African American men and 67% of African American women claimed to participate in little or no leisure time physical activity. The lack of exercise is an open door for diabetic complications.

Before beginning any diet or exercise program, however, consult with your doctor. Each case of diabetes is unique, and you many need extra "fuel" before any vigorous activity to maintain your blood glucose level. If you have Type 1 diabetes, insulin shots or pumps will be required throughout the day. For Type 2 diabetics, many can control their levels with diet and exercise, while others still take oral medication to help. Whatever your situation, you'll soon find that simple lifestyle changes can keep diabetes in check, while also improving your quality of life.

You're On

1. Which risk factors for diabetes can you identify in your life? If you have already been diagnosed with diabetes, skip this question.

_____

_____

_____

_____

2. Not only is cholesterol important as a risk factor for heart disease, it is also a risk factor for diabetes. So, how long has it been since you have had your cholesterol checked? Will you plan to have that done soon? (Remember that sometimes a local hospital, YMCA, or senior citizens center will offer this service).

_____

_____

_____

_____

_____

_____

3. What lifestyle changes will you make to minimize your risk or, if you are diabetic, help improve your life?

_____

_____

_____

_____

_____

_____

_____

_____

_____

_____

Supporting Roles

Websites

Diabetes.org

Diabetesnet.com

MayoClinic.com

Books

**The American Diabetes Association
Complete Guide to Diabetes**
American Diabetes Association
McGraw-Hill/Contemporary Distributed Products
3rd edition – November 2002

Betty Crocker's Diabetes Cookbook
Betty Crocker Editors
Betty Crocker
February 2003

The Diabetes Carbohydrate and Fat Gram Guide
Lea Ann Holzmeister
McGraw-Hill/Contemporary Distributed Products
2nd edition – March 2000

ACTION!

Based on what you have learned in this chapter, what are three concise, measurable, attainable goals you will set for yourself as you minimize your risk for diabetes? If you are already diabetic, what can you do to take better care of yourself? Be sure to include a schedule and target date for reaching each goal and a reward for accomplishing it.

1. Goal: _____

Schedule and target completion date: _____

Reward: _____

_____

2. Goal: _____

Schedule and target completion date: _____

Reward: _____

_____

3. Goal: _____

Schedule and target completion date: _____

Reward: _____

_____

14

The Lady and Breast Cancer

Introducing

God made you a woman — a "wonderfully made" woman, according to Psalm 139:14. In doing so, he made parts of you to be distinctly female — parts that inherently bring about your sense of womanhood. As these parts develop, so does your sense of being a woman. Likewise, an attack on these parts is an attack on your womanhood.

Welcome to the world of the woman battling breast cancer. Not only is this disease a physical onslaught, it is a barrage against your womanhood, your femininity, your natural beauty as a divinely designed leading lady. In its wake, it leaves you questioning your self-worth as a mother, a wife, a girlfriend, a professional woman, a sister, or simply a woman. Fortunately for every woman, breast cancer can be fought — and for most, it can be fought early. Learn in this chapter how to take care of your breasts, how to detect signs of an attack and how to reduce the overall risk of breast cancer.

While not every woman is a mother, God designed the breast as an expression of the nurturing character found in every woman. Do your best to extend this nurturing to yourself, and take care of the exclusively feminine gift God has given you.

The Main Event

Act 1: Facing the Facts

A very good friend of mine died from breast cancer this year. For more than 205,000 women this year, this terrible disease will attack the very core of their womanhood. Of these, more than 43,000 will die. It is the disease women fear the most, reaching one of every eight women in the United States and causing more deaths among women from ages 40 to 55 than any other cancer. Although the incidence of breast cancer has risen in the past two decades, the number of deaths from it has remained the same due to improved techniques of detection and treatment.

Despite this good news, there is concern for African American women. While you are generally less likely to get breast cancer than a Caucasian woman, the National Cancer Institute reports that you are 2.2 times more likely to die from the disease. A staggering 33% of black women diagnosed with breast cancer end up dying, compared to only 15% among Japanese women. Regardless of the reasons for these statistics, there is obviously cause for concern.

Yet there is also cause for hope; with newfound emphasis being placed on early detection through screenings and

Fortunately for every woman, breast cancer can be fought — and for most, it can be fought early.

more extensive research resulting in better treatment, the risk of breast cancer can be significantly reduced. Whereas 30 years ago, a diagnosis of breast cancer usually resulted in removal of the entire breast, today this treatment is the last resort and seldom occurs. With improved mammography, breast cancer can be detected as many as three years before a lump can even be felt. Out of every 1,000 mammograms, only one or two actually lead to a diagnosis of cancer.

Breast cancer is simply an abnormal growth of cells that form within the breast but can easily spread to other parts of the body. Most breast cancer incidents begin in the ducts of the breast, the channels that transfer milk to the nipple. (Only 10 to 15% of cases arise in the lobules, which are the actual milk-producing sacs.) There are many types of breast cancer, ranging from tubular carcinoma to ductal carcinoma in situ (DCIS) to more rare forms like inflammatory breast cancer.

It's important to note that not every lump you discover on your breasts is cancerous. Most, in fact, are benign and can be attributed to fibrocystic changes, which involve either fibrous connective tissue or the fluid-filled sacs called cysts. Often, these changes occur prior to a period, causing the breasts to swell, possibly emit a nipple discharge or feel painfully lumpy. While these signs are normal and certainly not life threatening, consult with your doctor if you feel you've discovered an abnormality.

> *With improved mammography, breast cancer can be detected as far as three years before a lump can even be felt. Out of every 1,000 mammograms, only one or two actually lead to a diagnosis of cancer.*

You're On

1. This year, how many women will be afflicted with breast cancer?

_____

_____

2. Out of every 1,000 mammograms, how many actually lead to a diagnosis of cancer?

_____

_____

3. What should you do if you discover an abnormality in your breast(s)?

_____

_____

_____

_____

_____

_____

_____

_____

_____

_____

Act 2: Addressing the Problem

Twenty-five years ago, the list of risk factors for breast cancer was short due to limited knowledge about the disease. Today, things have changed as both diagnosis and treatments have improved. But while the list has certainly expanded, most factors that cause breast cancer are still unknown, which is why the American Cancer Society estimates that almost 75% of incidents occur in women with no known risk factors. We do know, however, that the following factors increase your risk of breast cancer:

◆ excessive alcohol consumption

◆ active or passive tobacco smoke

◆ early age at onset of menses (when your period begins)

◆ late age at onset of menopause

◆ first full-term pregnancy after age 30

◆ family history of pre-menopausal breast cancer

◆ personal history of breast cancer or benign proliferative breast disease

◆ obesity or high dietary fat intake

◆ breast changes — atypical hyperplasia or lobular carcinoma in situ (LCIS) may increase a woman's risk for developing cancer

◆ genetic alteration — especially in changes to certain genes (BRCA1, BRCA2)

◆ exposure to estrogen

◆ breast density — breast cancers nearly always develop in lobular or ductal tissue (non-fatty tissue), which means a cancer is more likely to occur in breasts with a lot of this tissue than in breasts containing a lot of fatty tissue

◆ radiation therapy before age 30

◆ exposure to certain carcinogens (polycyclic aromatic hydrocarbons) emitted in cigarette smoke and charred red meat

At the top of this list, however, is one key factor: age. The older you get, the greater your risk of breast cancer. The disease rarely affects women under 30 years of age; by age 40, you have a one in 217 chance of developing breast cancer. Yet by age 85, those odds jump to one in eight. Almost 80% of breast cancers occur in women over age 50.

Although there is no surefire way to prevent breast cancer, the key to decreasing the risk of its attack is early detection. For cases that are detected because of observable symptoms, the cancer is more likely to be severe and have spread to other parts of the body. Thus, the sooner the cancer is detected, the greater the likelihood of a successful treatment.

There are three main ways to detect breast cancer early enough to minimize its harmfulness. The first is the easiest and most convenient, although not the most reliable. The breast self exam (BSE) involves a recommended monthly examination of your breasts and is done either seven to ten days from the beginning of your menstrual cycle or, if your periods are irregular, on the same day each month. The more familiar you become with the feel of your breasts, the more likely you will be able to detect any lumps or abnormalities. To conduct a BSE,

1. Stand in front of a mirror and inspect each breast separately. Note any asymmetry of size, contour, color, or shape.

2. Raise your hands over your head. Note any changes, particularly in the skin, such as wrinkling, dimpling, or retraction in a specific area.

3. Next, lie down with a pillow under your right shoulder and place your right arm behind your head, making sure your right breast is as evenly flattened against your chest as possible.

Almost 80% of breast cancers occur in women over age 50

4. Place the finger pads of the three middle fingers of your left hand on the outer part of your bare right breast.

5. Using small, dime-sized, circular motions without lifting your fingers, press first with light pressure, then with medium pressure, and finally with firm pressure. Start on the outermost part of your breast, move slowly inward toward the nipple, and make your way back to the starting point. You should be able to feel different layers of breast tissue using these different pressures. Make note of any masses or abnormalities that you feel. Avoid compressing your breast between your fingers, as it's possible to detect a "lump" that doesn't really exist.

6. Examine all areas of your breast and chest area from the collarbone to below the breast and including the armpit. You can also move your hands in lines, circles around the nipple or wedges from the nipple. Whichever method you choose, do it the same each time.

7. After fully examining your right breast, gently squeeze the nipple and look for any discharge.

8. Switch positions and examine your left breast in the same way.

While the BSE certainly isn't the most effective way for early detection of breast cancer, it familiarizes you with the natural feel of your breasts, therefore preparing you to more readily detect any abnormalities. Women are encouraged to begin the BSE as early as age 20. Any concerns from the examination should be voiced to your doctor.

Along with the BSE is the clinical breast examination (CBE), which is conducted by your doctor or health-care provider. This should be done every three years for women age 20 to 39 and annually for women 40 and up. If you have a family history of cancer or are at high risk for cancer because of other reasons, the CBE should be conducted more often. In this exam-ination, your doctor will examine your breast for lumps or other changes you may have missed during your BSE.

If you are age 40 or older, it is imperative that you get a yearly mammogram, as your risk for breast cancer drastically increases.

While the BSE and CBE are good meth-ods to alert you to the signs of breast cancer, a mammogram is the most effective tool today in detecting developing cancers impos-sible to discover by touch. A mammogram is simply a series of x-rays of the breast, which a radiologist will use to detect calcium deposits, masses, or changes in the breast foundation. Screening mammography involves two different views of each breast and is usually done for women with no risk factors or signs of breast problems. A mammogram takes only 20 minutes, with the actual breast compression (for taking the x-ray) lasting only a few seconds. The compression may feel uncomfortable, but you should not feel pain; if so, tell the technologist. (Note: If you are close to your period and your breasts are tender, schedule a mammogram for another day.)

If you are age 40 or older, it is imperative that you get a yearly mammogram, as your risk for breast cancer drastically increases. Women between the ages of 35 and 40 should have a baseline screening mammogram, and those with a family history of breast cancer should begin even earlier.

You're On

1. Which risk factors for breast cancer can you identify in your life? If you have already been diagnosed with breast cancer, skip this question.

_____

_____

_____

_____

_____

_____

2. How long has it been since you have had a mammogram?
Will you schedule one if you are overdue? Also, are you per-
forming BSE regularly? If not, will you start today?

_____

_____

_____

_____

_____

_____

3. What lifestyle changes will you make to minimize your
risk of breast cancer?

_____

_____

_____

_____

_____

_____

_____

Supporting Roles

Websites

Nationalbreastcancer.org

Breastcancer.org

Cancerfacts.com

MayoClinic.com

Books

Dr. Susan Love's Breast Book
Dr. Susan Love
Perseus Publishing
3rd revision edition – September 1999

The Breast Cancer Prevention Diet
Dr. Bob Arnot
Little, Brown and Co.
September 1999

The Breast Cancer Companion
(for those already diagnosed)
Kathy LaTour
Avon Books
Reprinted October 1994

ACTION!

*B*ased on what you have learned in this chapter, what are three concise, measurable, attainable goals you will set for yourself as you take responsibility for your breast health? Your goals might include beginning a routine BSE or making sure you get a mammogram when you are supposed to. Be sure to include a schedule and target date for reaching each goal and a reward for accomplishing it.

1. Goal: _____

Schedule and target completion date: _____

Reward: _____

_____

2. Goal: _____

Schedule and target completion date: _____

Reward: _____

_____

3. Goal: _____

Schedule and target completion date: _____

Reward: _____

_____

15

The Lady and S.T.D.s

Introducing

God designed sex to be an intimate expression of love between a husband and wife. It is private in nature, a bond existing only between the two who are one in marriage. Yet in a fallen world, the sacred boundaries of marital sex have been torn down, and sex is now the primary currency in a world starving for immediate pleasure — a fallen world that also suffers from disease, sickness, famine, and war.

For many Christians, this leaves the issue of sexually transmitted diseases (STDs) not only as a mystery (how can innocent children have AIDS?), but also as a taboo subject of discussion. Because the Bible mandates sex only within marriage, many believers are unsure about where to turn when they find themselves infected with an STD. Feelings of guilt and condemnation accompany the many questions that surface when facing an STD. But the reality is this: Because we live in a fallen world, everyone who is sexually active is susceptible to STDs — even husbands and wives who are faithful believers. With the rise of the HIV/AIDS virus, most of us now realize that the terms of contracting an STD have changed. Unfortunately, sexual activity is no longer the only way some of these diseases are transferred.

As with any disease, the key is to be alert and aware. Be alert by having a checkup. If you are an African American woman, you are part of the largest percentage of STD carriers, so consulting your doctor is important — if not essential. Be aware by understanding the risk factors that can lead to contracting an STD and doing all you can do to prevent that from occurring.

The Main Event

Act 1: Facing the Facts

In many ways, STDs are "silent killers" both because they can arise without detectable symptoms and because many people are unaware they're infected.

A sexually transmitted disease is a disease spread mainly by having sexual activity with someone who is infected. An STD (formally known as a venereal disease), however, can also be transferred via other non-sexual means such as contact with body fluids or its transmission from a mother to her newborn baby. Among all the STDs, there are two main causes: viruses (hepatitis B, herpes, HIV, HPV), which can be controlled but not cured, and bacteria (chlamydia, gonorrhea, syphilis), which can be cured. While many of us have limited knowledge about these diseases, most of us have sensed the stigma surrounding them. Yet as taboo as STDs can be in the Christian culture, statistics prove both their frequency and severity.

An estimated 65 million-plus Americans have one of the 20 identified STDs, with 15 million new cases arising each year. That's an astonishing one in five people — certainly a cause for concern. In many ways, STDs are "silent killers" both because they can arise without detectable symptoms and because many people are unaware they're infected. As an example, it's estimated that as many as one in four Americans has genital herpes, yet only 20% of those infected are actually aware they have it. Twenty-five percent of Americans will contract an STD at some point during their lifetime.

Unfortunately, the news gets worse for African American women. An alarming 46% of all black women have herpes, compared to only 18% of white women. Both the gonorrhea and syphilis rates among African American women are more than 30 times higher than they are among Caucasian women, with almost 9% of all black women being infected by gonorrhea. Likewise, the number of HIV virus cases continues to increase among African American women at an alarming rate. There is good news, however: The syphilis rate among black women has significantly declined. While almost two-thirds of all cases still involve African Americans, the overall rate has decreased by almost 30% in recent years.

While many STDs are incurable, many can be cured, if detected early. The difficulty with detection, however, is that many STDs do not have clear symptoms, especially with women. And when symptoms are evident, they are often mistaken for those of a nonsexual disease. Because of this, women who have had more than one sex partner in the past should be screened or tested periodically

Among all these facts, it seems one stands out as the most telling: Two-thirds of all STDs occur in people 25 years old and younger. Twenty-five percent of all new cases involve teenagers. Yet almost half of adults from ages 18 to 44 have never been tested for an STD other than HIV/AIDS. While many STDs are incurable, many can be cured, if detected early. The difficulty with detection, however, is that many STDs do not have clear symptoms, especially with women. And when symptoms are evident, they are often mistaken for those of a nonsexual disease. Because of this, women who have had more than one sex partner in the past should be screened or tested periodically.

Here are a few symptoms that are common and detectible among STDs:

- burning sensation in the urethra when urinating
- canker sores (painful red sores) on the genital area, anus, tongue and/or throat
- small blisters that turn into scabs on the genital area
- soft, flesh-colored warts around the genital area
- abnormal discharge from the vagina
- itching or soreness around the vagina
- recurring yeast infections
- itching, pain, or discharge in the anal area
- redness, swelling, bumps, or rashes in the genital or anal area
- pain in the pelvic or abdominal area
- pain, soreness, irritation, or other discomfort during intercourse

- bleeding after intercourse
- sore throats (only among those who have oral sex)
- scaly rash on the palms of your hands and the soles of your feet
- dark urine; loose, light-colored stools; and yellow eyes and skin
- swollen glands, fever, and body aches
- unusual infections, unexplained fatigue, night sweats, and weight loss

You're On

1. What are the two main causes of STDs?

_____

_____

_____

_____

2. About how many Americans are infected with STDs?

_____

_____

213

3. What are five symptoms of an STD?

_____

_____

_____

_____

_____

Act 2: Addressing the Problem

Unfortunately, women often suffer from the most severe health problems related to sexually transmitted diseases (STDs), largely because they often confuse STD symptoms with typical non-STD infections. Yet STDs can cause any of the following among women:

◆ pelvic inflammatory disease (PID), which can cause chronic pelvic pain, infertility and ectopic pregnancy (pregnancy outside the uterus, which can be fatal)

◆ cervical cancer

◆ death

◆ transference of an STD from mother to newborn baby. (This can even permanently disable or kill the newborn.)

The fact is that if you've ever had sex, you're a candidate for having an STD. Although the specific risk factors vary for each STD, your risk for contracting an STD increases with any of the following factors:

◆ sex with multiple sexual partners

◆ sex with someone else who had multiple sexual partners

◆ sex without using a condom

◆ age — sexually active teenagers and young women are more at risk (for instance, they're more prone to chlamydia because of the makeup of cells lining the cervical canal)

◆ improper use of a condom for sexual protection

◆ pregnancy — pregnant women are at increased risk for complications of both bacterial vaginosis and chlamydia

◆ anal sex

◆ douching (increased risk for bacterial vaginosis)

◆ use of intrauterine device (IUD) for contraception

◆ poor nutrition and hygiene (increased risk for genital warts)

Women often suffer from the most severe health problems related to sexually transmitted diseases (STDs).

When you disregard these risks, you open yourself up to any of the following possible problems:

◆ Chlamydia can lead to infertility, cancer of the cervix, HIV infection, proctitis (an infection of the lining of the rectum), and eye infection or blindness

◆ Syphilis can lead to paralysis, mental problems, heart damage, blindness, or death

◆ Bacterial vaginosis can lead to pelvic inflammatory disease (PID), infertility, ectopic pregnancy, HIV infection, and low birth weight or early delivery (for pregnant women)

◆ Gonorrhea can lead to infertility and infection in the heart, skin, joints (arthritis), or eyes, causing blindness

◆ HIV/AIDS can lead to opportunistic infections (life-threatening diseases) and various forms of cancer

◆ Genital herpes if acquired during pregnancy, can lead to a transmission of the virus to newborn baby, which eventually can lead to mental retardation or death of baby

While these are just a few possible extreme results, they are nonetheless proven results if STDs are left untreated or uncured. To avoid this, the first and most important thing to do is to see your doctor. Whether you have STD symptoms or not, ask for a checkup to test whether you have any STDs. If you are diagnosed with one, it's essential to tell your partner. Abstain from any sexual activity immediately, and communicate openly and honestly about past sexual encounters, if any, for the sake of discovering when the disease could have been contracted. You must also both be treated to prevent becoming re-infected. It's also important to remember that common birth control methods such as the contraceptive pill, shot or implant don't protect you from STDs. Condoms are still the only way to protect you from STDs, although they do not provide complete protection.

Along with these tips, you can take the following pre-cautions to avoid contracting an STD:

◆ Abstain from all sexual activity.

◆ Wash your genitals with soap and water, and urinate after you have sex.

◆ If you or your partner has recently had sex with someone else, use a condom for any sexual activity.

◆ Avoid contact with body fluids, body tissues, or open sores.

◆ Have regular checkups for STDs.

◆ Stay mutually monogamous with one uninfected sexual partner.

◆ Use clean needles if injecting intravenous drugs, and only under a doctor's orders.

◆ Avoid having sex during menstruation. (Women infected with the HIV virus are more likely to spread the virus, while non-infected women are more susceptible to getting infected during their period.)

◆ Avoid anal intercourse.

◆ Avoid douching.

◆ If you've recently given birth, check with your doctor about the possible risk of transmission of an STD in your breast milk.

◆ Avoid using N-9, a spermicide contraceptive that can cause vaginal lesions.

> *Remember that common birth control methods such as the contraceptive pill, shot, or implant don't protect you from STDs. Condoms are still the only way to protect you from STDs, although they do not provide complete protection.*

◆ Use condoms correctly, meaning a condom should be put on the penis before beginning sex and not taken off until withdrawal. If this is not possible, consider using a female condom.

Sexually transmitted diseases can be frightening, embarrassing, and deadly. If you know you have one, avoid the temptation to keep quiet; it's crucial that you consult your doctor and tell your sexual partner. Undetected, many more complications can arise. Whether you're uncertain about having an STD or not, it's essential to see a doctor for a checkup on a regular basis. You not only protect yourself, you also protect the health of others.

You're On

1. Are you — or have you ever been — at risk for any STD's (Remember, anyone who is sexually active is at risk.)? If so, have you spoken with your doctor about this? When will you do so?

_____

_____

_____

_____

_____

_____

2. Are you living in holiness when it comes to your sex life? In other words, are you practicing sex only within marriage?

_____

_____

_____

_____

_____

_____

_____

_____

_____

_____

3. If you have or carry an STD, are you being responsible and following the doctor's orders?

_____

_____

_____

_____

_____

Supporting Roles

Websites

Clubvarsity.org

Thebody.com

Urologychannel.com

Book

Sexually Transmitted Diseases:
A Physician Tells You What You Need to Know
Lisa Marr
Johns Hopkins Press
December 1998

ACTION!

*B*ased on what you have learned in this chapter, what are three concise, measurable, attainable goals you will set for yourself in the area of your sexual health? If you may be at risk for an STD and haven't had a check-up, one of your goals could be to make that appointment (and keep it!). Be sure to include a schedule and target date for reaching each goal and a reward for accomplishing it.

1. Goal: _____

Schedule and target completion date: _____

Reward: _____

_____

2. Goal: _____

Schedule and target completion date: _____

Reward: _____

_____

3. Goal: _____

Schedule and target completion date: _____

Reward: _____

_____

Appendix A: Goals at a Glance

Take a few moments to review the goals you set for yourself in the Action! sections at the end of each chapter and compile them on the lines below. Group them by chapters, beginning with chapter one, using one blank for each goal. For example, list each of your three goals from Chapter 1 on the blanks next to Number 1 — using one blank for each goal. Then for every chapter's goals, put a star or a circle around the one that is most important to you. This will help you set your priorities. You might want to consider keeping that short list of most important goals in your appointment book, on your daily calendar, or posting it on your refrigerator.

Chapter 1   1. _____   2. _____   3. _____

Chapter 2   1. _____   2. _____   3. _____

Chapter 3   1. _____   2. _____   3. _____

Chapter 4   1. _____   2. _____   3. _____

Chapter 5   1. _____   2. _____   3. _____

Chapter 6   1. _____   2. _____   3. _____

Chapter 7   1. _____   2. _____   3. _____

Chapter 8   1. _____   2. _____   3. _____

Chapter 9   1. _____   2. _____   3. _____

Chapter 10   1. _____   2. _____   3. _____

Chapter 11   1. _____   2. _____   3. _____

Chapter 12   1. _____   2. _____   3. _____

Chapter 13   1. _____   2. _____   3. _____

Chapter 14   1. _____   2. _____   3. _____

Chapter 15   1. _____   2. _____   3. _____

Appendix B: Making Wise Food Choices

The lists below will help you in your commitment to take care of yourself by eating right. This page can be cut out and taped onto your refrigerator or placed somewhere else where you can view it easily when you are making decisions about what to eat.

Don't

◆ Use whole or 2 % milk

◆ Eat sausage, bacon, veal, or pork

◆ Use butter and margarine

◆ Use shortening

◆ Eat many cheeses

◆ Eat donuts, sweet rolls, or muffins regularly

◆ Use whole sour cream

◆ Eat fried foods

◆ Choose "dark meat" turkey and chicken

◆ Eat foods containing synthetic sugars

Do

◆ Eat whole grain products

◆ Eat lots of vegetables and fruits

◆ Use low-fat dairy products

◆ Choose lean cuts of meat, especially poultry and fish

◆ Use herbs and yogurt as seasonings instead of butter, shortening, or sour cream.

◆ Prepare meat by baking, broiling, and roasting, the healthiest ways to prepare meat. Lean cuts can be pan-broiled or stir-fried.

◆ Always use a nonstick pan and nonstick cooking spray instead of bacon fat or butter when cooking meats or eggs.

◆ Trim outside fat on meats before cooking. Trim any inside, separable fat before eating. In poultry, most of the fat is located under the skin, so you can reduce additional fat by removing the skin.

◆ Use herbs, spices, fresh vegetables, and nonfat marinades to season meat. Avoid high-fat sauces and gravies. Avoid also high sodium marinades and high sodium dry rub seasonings.

◆ Prepare fish by poaching, steaming, baking, and broiling. Check your fish to make sure it's fresh. It should have firm, springy flesh, a clear color, a moist look, and a clean smell.

◆ When selecting meats, choose lean ones such as turkey or chicken breasts. Lean beef and veal cuts have the word "loin" or "round" in their names; lean pork cuts have the word "loin" or "leg" in their names.

◆ Drastically reduce or eliminate synthetic sugars (found in most desserts, baked goods, processed snacks, and candies) from your diet. Instead, choose vegetables and fruits that are low in fat and also contain fiber, vitamins, and minerals.

◆ Build your meals around vegetables, fruits, and whole-grain products, and lighten up on the meat and dairy products.

Notes

Notes

Notes

Notes

Notes

Notes

Notes

Notes

Notes

Notes

Notes

Notes

Notes

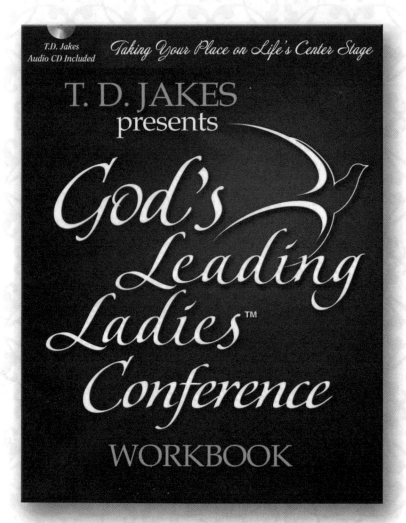